T0035161

EXTRAORDINARY HEARING

Preparing Your Soul to Hear from God

GREG PRUETT

A Tyndale nonfiction imprint

Visit Tyndale online at tyndale.com.

Visit Tyndale Momentum online at tyndalemomentum.com.

Extraordinary Hearing: Preparing Your Soul to Hear from God

Designed by Libby Dykstra

Edited by Steve Halliday

Italics in Scripture quotations reflect the author's emphasis.

For information about special discounts for bulk purchases, please contact Tyndale House Publishers at csresponse@tyndale.com, or call 1-855-277-9400.

Library of Congress Cataloging-in-Publication Data

A catalog record for this book is available from the Library of Congress.

ISBN 978-1-4964-6685-3

Printed in the United States of America

29 28 27 26 25 24 23
7 6 5 4 3 2 1

I dedicate this book to the seldom-celebrated men and women of faith who dependably serve the Church. I respect your courage and honesty to ask genuine questions about your moments of spiritual dissonance. Like Jacob, you grapple with God in an epic struggle to make sense of the physical and spiritual challenges of earthly life.

You never tire of undergirding the work of Jesus and His Church with powerful, sustaining prayer. You help unswervingly both saints and sinners alike. You think yourselves average, yet the Church relies on your devotion every day.

I never knew how many in the Church strive audaciously every day to understand and practice prayer until I wrote a book about it—and unexpectedly became the recipient of your queries and ideas. Your insightful questions have led me to puzzle out this writing. Your conundrums inspire my creativity. Surely glory awaits you in heaven beyond your wildest imagination!

CONTENTS

FOREWORD

FOR SEVERAL YEARS I've worked with many people to try to speed up the translation of the Bible into more than six thousand of the vital languages spoken on our planet. Our projections showed the work would not be finished until 2150.

And then another voice spoke. It said we could get the job done by 2033.

Was this the voice of God leading us? Or was it man-made? To eliminate more than a century from the target would take extraordinary hearing, for sure!

Greg Pruett entered my life as we set out on this grand and daunting adventure for the Kingdom of God. I knew that Greg, as president of Pioneer Bible Translators, would need to feel led to join our effort if we were to have any chance at all of eradicating "Bible poverty" on our watch. From the earliest days, I also knew that if we were going to meet our goal, it would take extreme prayer, the kind Greg wrote about in his first book. Throughout this initiative, Greg has been a strong champion for prayer, reminding us of its centrality and power. When we set up a prayer task force to coordinate the efforts of all eleven Bible translation partners, Greg was picked to lead the group.

It has been a joy to meet with Greg, our ten other Bible translator CEO partners, as well as the four other resource partners involved with illumiNations, to strategize our "big, hairy, audacious goal." Most of our monthly meetings have taken place in the Admirals Club at Gate C20 of the Dallas/Fort Worth airport.

Now that I've read Greg's new manuscript, I have to ask: Did we, in fact, hear God speak about our Bible translation goal? I believe so, but as we rush toward 2033, we will see for sure.

As you read *Extraordinary Hearing*, you will note the extremely practical nature of the ideas unpacked in this book. Greg does not speak or write theoretically; he describes real-world experiences that have brought him and his wife, Rebecca, to where they are today. The principles he shares have immediate, this-world application, with the power to change all our lives for the better.

Another highlight for me is Greg's mischievous sense of humor, wrapped around the stories he tells and the lessons he brings out of them. Meeting regularly with Greg over the past decade has enabled me to hear his voice and appreciate his distinctive sense of humor, even as I read his words. And he writes so descriptively! At one point as I read the manuscript, I grabbed my wife and said, "Listen to this!" We both smiled as I read aloud a paragraph from this unique, new book, pleased and gratified to hear Greg explain a key issue with such skill and grace.

Even the title he chose, *Extraordinary Hearing*, hits the mark. Look up the word *extraordinary* in the dictionary and it will define the term like this: "going beyond what is usual." Look up the word *hearing* in that same dictionary and it will say, "the process, function, or power of perceiving sound." Put them together and you have "going beyond what is usual in the process, function, or power of perceiving sound."[1]

And that is *precisely* the adventure you are about to embark on in this book.

In the following pages, Greg will help you to understand the process, function, and power of extraordinary hearing—the ability and skill it takes to accurately hear God's voice and distinguish it from a host of other voices.

I trust that as you read *Extraordinary Hearing*, you, too, will grow in your ability to hear God's voice . . . and then obey whatever you hear!

The Bible is alive,

Mart Green
Founder of Mardel Christian and Education;
ministry investment officer at Hobby Lobby
August 2022

INTRODUCTION

God Is Calling

THE FIRST TIME God spoke to me, I was sitting inside a dark storage cabinet. Hear me out on this; don't judge me yet.

I found it nearly impossible to get alone back at Texas A&M University in 1987. Twenty-four hours a day, my roommate played records by the drug culture band the Moody Blues. He also slept with a throwing knife in his hand, which kept me on edge. So to pray, I would slip over to the All Faiths Chapel, a church-like, glass structure that most students rigorously avoided. The decision to seek God in that quiet place of prayer changed everything for me.

While I prayed there, a mysterious, quiet student with striking, blue eyes attracted my attention. Most days she would play the piano and sing worship songs for a long time. She seemed to embody the stillness and spirituality I was chasing after—and I might have wanted to pursue some other qualities she had, too, but this story isn't about that right now.

One day while on my knees in the chapel trying to connect with God, even in the stillness of that austere place of worship, something about praying with a few people walking around felt a bit too public for me to concentrate. I attended InterVarsity Christian Fellowship at the time, which had a cabinet in the back of the chapel used for storing Bibles, hymnals, and boxes of the Gospel of John suitable for mass distribution. The cabinet stood just a foot and a half off the ground, built into a wall.

Back then, people talked about going into your "prayer closet." So one day, feeling the intense need to get alone with God, I climbed up into that cabinet, sat down on a box, and deftly pulled the door closed without smashing my fingers.

Delicious darkness swallowed me. I remember the smooth, dusty feel of cardboard boxes all around and the reassuringly religious smell of musty hymnals. I reveled in the quiet hour I spent there, the supreme silence you find only in an isolated closet inside a ghostly still chapel. I knew right away I had found my prayer place. From then on, I often passed a blissful hour pouring out my soul before God's throne, right there in the dark of that cabinet.

It felt heavenly . . . except on those rare occasions when someone from InterVarsity would swing by for supplies and the door sprang open with a crash of brilliant light. As my eyes adjusted, squinting like a raccoon caught in a porch light, I saw the wide-eyed expression of shock sweep over the person's face. Then, little by little, shock would give way to stunned bewilderment. Next, as they came to grasp that a student had inexplicably perched himself in the cabinet, it got awkward. No social etiquette exists for what to do when someone discovers you praying in a storage cabinet.

Perhaps I should have confidently reached over and offered the person a hymnal, as though I were hunched up there for just that purpose. I especially liked when they abruptly slammed the door shut, apparently realizing they had committed some terrible social sin—in the process plunging me back into the inky darkness.

It was worth it.

The Day God Spoke to Me

I remember the day God clearly spoke to me. One moment I lifted up a concern to the Lord, and the next I heard in my mind urgent words not of my own design: "*While you still can!*" I stumbled out of the darkness that day, troubled by what I had "heard."

I didn't hear a sound caught by the ear, but instead a thought coming from outside myself. At first I wondered, *Does "While you still can" mean my time on earth is short?* That didn't seem to fit. Everyone's time is short. As the words replayed in my mind, it dawned on me that, when you waste an opportunity in this life, you never get it back. We who follow Jesus must take action "while we still can."

Jesus said it this way: "As long as it is day, we must do the works of him who sent me. Night is coming, when no one can work" (John 9:4). When I saw the same idea written in the Word, I came to understand that I had indeed heard the Lord, a repeat of a message already written in the Bible two thousand years ago.

I now realize that this moment gave me my calling. The eyes

of the Lord had ranged "throughout the earth to strengthen those whose hearts are fully committed to him" (2 Chronicles 16:9). When He looked over at Texas A&M University in 1987, He saw a naive college kid whispering in a dark closet and said to a nearby angel, "Hey, watch this." With just the four words "*While you still can*," He laid claim to my whole life. From that moment, I knew one thing for sure: I must waste no time in pursuing my purpose. God had made me *for* something.

The words make sense now. God could glance down the pathways of time and see that I would marry Rebecca, the intriguing beauty playing the chapel piano. He could see that she would influence me to abandon my career ideas and become a Bible translator, the dream she had pursued and prayed about while she played. He knew the long process ahead of me, something that would take decades. He knew I would eventually become a leader in a Bible agency at the exact moment in history when we would have the chance to start the last Bible translation projects needed. His first words to me therefore became a resounding command not to mess around. He telegraphed the future for me, that I would need to focus if I were to realize my created purpose.

Those words crashed into my life like thunder. I recognized in that message an opportunity to give myself away to Him forever. I still mist up whenever I remember it. Nothing like it happened again for a very long time.

What If You Could Hear Him?

What if *you* could hear God speaking? What difference would that make in your life? I don't mean hearing an audible voice. I wouldn't need to write a book about hearing *that*. You would just listen. Instead, I mean receiving a message from Him as a thought in the mind. Deaf people also have access to this kind of "hearing" because our powerful God can speak into any human mind in any language, including sign language.

The listening I'm pursuing, the hearing I have in mind, refers to receiving internal guidance from God, the leading of the Holy Spirit deep within us.

Such hearing used to be limited to a few prophets gifted with the Spirit. But now all of us who follow Jesus have access to that same Spirit. Hearing God is not only a *possibility* but also a *necessity* if we want to serve Him well. We need the instructions that Isaiah described: "Your own ears will hear him. Right behind you a voice will say, 'This is the way you should go,' whether to the right or to the left" (Isaiah 30:21, NLT). We need the fellowship that Jesus promised: "Here I am! I stand at the door and knock. If anyone *hears my voice* and opens the door, I will come in and eat with that person, and they with me" (Revelation 3:20).* He would not have told the church at Laodicea to listen for His voice at the door if no voice was coming.

Wouldn't life be so much more efficient with God's instructions? Couldn't we get more work accomplished investing four hours a day following God's marching orders than we could in a ten-hour workday under our own wisdom? How much sweat and energy have we poured down a hole, like vanishing gallons of water, as we pursue fruitless ideas and counterproductive dreams, when we could instead focus our lives on doing *exactly* what God created us to do under His direct guidance?

Ah, but how can we know it's really Him speaking?

---

* *Italics* in Scripture quotations reflect the author's emphasis.

Has God Finished Speaking?

I grew up in a relatively conservative church whose leaders *mostly* taught me that God had finished speaking once He revealed the Bible. He said everything He had to say when the perfect Word of God came to exist, they insisted.

Were you taught the same thing? Fortunately, I owe a debt of gratitude to my spiritual forebears because they also taught me to believe and treasure the Bible above all human input, even theirs.

Real theological turbulence in my life started when I did what they taught me to do: I actually read the Bible. The God in the Bible seemed much more talkative than I had learned growing up.

Then I went to college and came under the influence of people who seemed to hear from God all the time. I had never known charismatic Christians. Their habits impressed me. I observed them for a time and recognized that they seemed to regard their impressions and impulses as the word of the Lord.

One night, while I was at the church building studying for an engineering test, a fellow student brought me a paragraph written by Cliff, her friend with the gift of prophecy. She spoke softly as she reverently held out a small scrap of paper. "Greg," she announced, "Cliff just prophesied the word of the Lord!" I read it and nodded appreciatively while inspecting the words. "Good," I said.

Dumbfounded by my lack of enthusiasm, she waved the paper around in front of my eyes and declared more emphatically, "You don't understand! *This* is the word of the Lord!" I gave it a second look, no doubt unable to keep the skepticism off of my face.

They seemed like good words, but I didn't plan to staple

them into the back of my Bible or anything. I tried to drum up *some* enthusiasm, but I managed only to keep nodding, keep looking down at the paper, and keep repeating my original unsatisfactory remark: "Good."

I thought, *Maybe this is really it! Could it be that impulses during prayer really are the way to hear from God?*

But as an engineering student, I tested out the idea first. I would pray and then write down any strong impressions that came to me in prayer. I thought, *The word of the Lord has come.* But then I mused, *Of course, if these impulses truly are from God, the real world around me will conform to these messages.* I wrote them down carefully and watched to see whether they would come to pass. My tests proved them to be wholly unreliable.

I had not yet learned to recognize God's voice.

For the most part, I found that impulses are just impulses—truly important information for impulsive college students. We really need to *know* that God has spoken before we act on it. I do not want to live in a world of a pretend God whose voice I only imagine! I suspect the same is true for you.

Longing to Know Him

I long to truly know the Creator of this awesome universe. I don't want to make Him up. I want Him to rip open my world and clear up my muddled thinking and teach me how to thrive in this universe He made. I hunger for Him to hand me a great work to perform that will please Him. I crave walking in the brilliance of His presence each day as I live my life. I yearn to talk to the Mind great enough to stretch stars across the sky and meticulous enough to handcraft molecules. And I desperately wish to hear Him speak to me.

I think He created me with this craving deep inside, like

Adam walking in the cool of the Garden with God, just to pass time together in peace and quiet satisfaction. As I pray, I don't want just to get things from God. I want *God*! It's not enough for me to gallop after every errant impulse that enters my mind in prayer.

Sometimes in life, as in the Bible, a fine line exists between prophecy and lunacy. We can find it hard to tell the difference. In the twentieth chapter of Isaiah, we learn that the Lord instructed the prophet to go about his business, naked, for three years. I'm not making this up! Understandably, it's the shortest chapter in Isaiah by far, as if he couldn't bear to dwell on it. While I'm not above embarrassing my kids for the sake of a great sermon illustration, that has to be level two. But then again, God did tell Isaiah to name one of his kids Quick-to-the-Plunder-Quick-To-Destroy (Isaiah 8:3).[2] How embarrassing in middle school! I had a toddler like that, too, but I didn't put *that* on her birth certificate.

I imagine that Isaiah's kids looked back on that phase of their dad's ministry as "the naked years." Worst of all, God put him through all of that humiliation just to drive home a prophetic point that, from my limited human perspective, Isaiah could have made quite sufficiently by speaking a couple of sentences in a Speedo swimsuit.

We do not serve a safe, ordinary God.

That's why we need to tread carefully as we learn to hear Him speak so that we can know for sure we are *really* hearing from God. We should expect that occasionally the word of the Lord could shock us, as in Isaiah 20. But we must not end up following equally embarrassing impulses from our own erratic neural synapses. For that reason, the first chapter of this book starts by basing our conversation on the rock-solid foundation of Scripture.

Discussion Questions

1. How comfortable do you feel with the idea that God could still speak to you?
2. Why do you believe that He does? Or why not?
3. If you can, describe a time when you believe God may have spoken to you or when the Holy Spirit directed you to do something.
4. How could you tell whether it was God speaking to you?
5. Do you feel a need for God to speak clearly into your life? Explain.
6. About what kinds of things in your life would you like God to guide you?

PART 1

EXTRAORDINARY HEARING IN THE BIBLE

CHAPTER 1

GOD SPEAKS

In those days the word of the LORD was rare;
there were not many visions.

I SAMUEL 3:I

THE LAMPLIGHT JUST started to dim on the face of the young boy tossing and turning in his bed inside the Tabernacle. Ever since his third birthday, Samuel had slept just on the other side of the veil from the Ark of the Covenant—literally in the presence of God. Back when his mother first gave him to God, he could fall asleep only by the golden lampstand's precious pool of light. Now that he was twelve, the dark no longer scared him. Even so, on nights when he brooded about how much he missed his mom, that lamp's light held back a different darkness.

As the tent gradually filled with shifting shadows, he made the mistake of rolling over in bed to face the cloth veil hiding the holiest place. Instantly his mind filled with the temptation to sneak a peek under the curtain to see the forbidden space and the smooth, golden box with imposing angelic figures fashioned on top, glittering with gold. He thought with a shiver about Eli's stern warning not to slip under the curtain into the Holy of Holies, for fear that he might touch the Ark of the Lord and die right there on the spot. He hadn't slept for a week after that lecture.

He was wondering what would happen if he crept over to the table across from the lampstand to snitch a bit of sacrificial bread when sleep stole over him. He dozed off at last.

Suddenly a voice broke the silence of the darkness. "Samuel!" it exclaimed.

His eyes instantly snapped open.

Eli must need something, he mused as he popped out of bed with the springy step of a young boy. He sprinted over to interrupt the slumber of the elderly priest.

"I didn't call you," Eli grumbled. "Go back to bed." For some reason, Eli always seemed grumpy at night. Samuel returned to his bed and tried to go back to sleep.

"Samuel!"

The second time he scampered even faster. Surely this time Eli wouldn't deny he had called him. But wow, was Eli ever upset!

"Go back and lie down! I didn't call you," Eli groused again. Samuel turned to go, a little slower this time, as a long, frustrated sigh rose from Eli's bed behind him.

Samuel felt truly puzzled. As he slipped back into his bed among the imposing articles of worship, he could not sleep. He had just settled in for a long night of staring in terror at the cloth of the ceiling when it happened for the third time.

"Samuel!"

He reluctantly crept into Eli's bedroom one last time, peering quietly to see if, by any chance, Eli waited for his arrival. But instead of anger, he saw that Eli's eyes had grown wide with recognition.

After all these many years of silence, could it really be? Eli thought with wonder.

"Samuel," he instructed, "next time when you hear the voice, say 'Speak, LORD, I'm listening and at your service'" (1 Samuel 3:9, GPT[†]).

No sooner had Samuel lain back down in bed than the sheer weight of a presence as vast as space pressed on his consciousness from the other side of the curtain. God came and stood in that dark tent between the golden Ark and the wide-eyed boy.

The Creator of the universe earnestly called: "Samuel! Samuel!" This time, the boy's soul had a ready answer: "Speak, because I'm listening and at your service." And then Samuel heard words that changed everything: "Listen, I am about to make a move in Israel so stunning it will ring in everyone's ears like a bell when they hear about it" (1 Samuel 3:11, GPT). With those words began the ministry of one of the great prophets of the Bible.

God Talks

The God of the Bible speaks to people. He has things to say, and He loves people so passionately that He just can't keep His plans to Himself. Our God is not one to keep His mouth shut! For some reason, at least with some mysteries, it simply isn't in His nature to keep a secret.

[†] When I want to highlight a nuance that other English translations might obscure, I use my own, which I playfully call the GPT (Greg Pruett Translation).

It doesn't surprise me that God would talk to a boy. But it shocks me that He had remained silent for a long time before that: "In those days, the word of the LORD was scarce. Visions just weren't appearing" (1 Samuel 3:1, GPT). Imagine how hard it must have felt for a God who loves conversation to hold His silence! The people who should have longed to walk and talk with Him instead busied themselves to get rich. Samuel's ministry changed all that.

One person plus God can become a powerful combination when people learn to listen. The Bible explains it this way: "The LORD was with Samuel as he grew up, and he let none of Samuel's words fall to the ground" (1 Samuel 3:19). What would that be like, for every word you say to count?

As I write this book, I long for you and me to learn to get so in tune to walking with God that every word we write or speak would soar brilliantly into the sky to become true and reliable, useful in the hands of God. We who serve the Lord desire to have a life like Samuel, so enveloped by God's presence that not a single utterance passes our lips, only to crash uselessly in the dirt.

God Explains

God talks *a lot* in the Bible. He made Adam and Eve apparently so that He could walk and chat with them in the cool of the Garden (Genesis 2:19; 3:8-9). Even after sin entered the world, some people still walked and talked with God.

Enoch walked with God for three hundred years, and, perhaps, God considered him such a riveting conversationalist that He took him away. No one saw Enoch on earth again (Genesis 5:24). Noah also "walked with God," modeling a just lifestyle and living above reproach (Genesis 6:9, ESV). One day as God and Noah walked and talked, God explained His plans: "So, Noah, I want you to know that I'm about to put an end to everything alive." That's the kind of thing God says in a chat. Then through a flood, He destroyed a world that had grown violent and corrupt.

Throughout the Bible, God talks with His people about the big moves He's about to make. He upended Abraham's life with a command and a sweeping, global promise: "All peoples on earth will be blessed through you" (Genesis 12:3). God thinks His chosen people have a right and a need to hear His thoughts. One day He said, "Shall I hide from Abraham what I am about to do? . . . For I have chosen him" (Genesis 18:17, 19). Then He and Abraham spent the next minutes debating the fate of the city of Sodom. It mattered to God what Abraham said in that conversation because He had chosen him. And God has chosen us too.

Later, God spoke to Jacob, switching his name to Israel because Jacob was the kind of man who wrestled with people and with God—and who came out on top (Genesis 32:28). That's how Jacob's descendants, the people of God, became known as "Israel." Those who struggle with God, His nature, and His plans—that's our true identity. We who follow the spiritual heritage of Israel find ourselves grappling with God with all our might, striving to get a grip on who He is and why He made us.

Later, God spoke to Moses through, of all things, a burning bush (Exodus 3:2). Moses' friendly conversations with God grew so frequent that he had to erect a special conference tent outside the camp just for consulting with the Creator. Everyone in the camp watched intently as a pillar of cloud descended on the tent, and Moses would go inside to listen and talk. Sooner or later, of course, Moses would have to come out and do the hard work of leading Israel (Exodus 33:7-11).

Joshua, however, refused to leave the tent (Exodus 33:11). He became qualified to replace Moses as leader by continually dwelling in this "Tent of Meeting" in God's presence. The Holy Place of the Tabernacle at the center of the camp later replaced the function of the Tent of Meeting and sometimes was still called the Tent of Meeting. The Temple later replaced the Tabernacle, but the Holy Place remained a space where God and priests would encounter one another (Luke 1:11). The first place of worship did not give God's people a location to meet one another. It was a place where God met and talked to His people.

God Warns through Dreams

From almost the very beginning, God has spoken through dreams.

- He cautioned Abimelech in a dream: "You are a dead man because you took a married woman from her husband" (Genesis 20:3, GPT).
- Jacob saw angels on a stairway to heaven at Bethel and inherited the divine promise from the figure standing at the top (Genesis 28:12-15).
- In a dream, God scared Laban to death, warning, "Watch yourself so you don't say a word to Jacob—either good or bad" (Genesis 31:24, GPT).
- He sent dreams to Pharaoh so that He could use Joseph to save His people from starvation in a famine (Genesis 41:25-27).
- He appeared to Solomon in a dream to let him choose the future of his reign (1 Kings 3:5).

- He saved baby Jesus from Herod by forewarning both the wise men and Joseph in a dream (Matthew 2:12-13).
- Pilate's wife told him to leave Jesus alone because she had been warned in a dream (Matthew 27:19).
- Daniel explained the purpose of dreams: "There is a God in heaven who reveals mysteries" (Daniel 2:28).

God Reveals Truth in Pictures

God shows His people visions too. Biblical visions take at least two forms, either something seen with the eye or a mental image from God. Often, we don't know which one happened (see 2 Corinthians 12:1-4).

One day God twice asked Jeremiah, "What do you see?" Jeremiah simply said, "I see the branch of an almond tree" and "I see a pot that is boiling." Another time God asked the same question and received the answer, "figs" (Jeremiah 1:11,13; 24:3).

God asked Zechariah, "What do you see?" But Zechariah saw far more complex pictures than Jeremiah (Zechariah 4:2; 5:2).

Amos got the same question a couple of times, but he saw a plumb line and a basket of fruit (Amos 7:8; 8:1-2). Each time, the visions captured spiritual meaning in symbols that the prophet was expected to proclaim.

God speaks indirectly through visions so that people will think hard to figure out what He's saying. God shocked Peter with a vision of "unclean" animals coming down from heaven, beasts that God had forbidden Jews to eat. God commanded Peter to break the law by eating those animals. Later, the meaning dawned on Peter: "I now realize how true it is that God does not show favoritism" (Acts 10:34).

God Poses Questions

God asks his people probing questions:[3]

> Adam, where are you? (Genesis 3:9)
> Cain, why are you angry? (Genesis 4:6)
> Abraham, why did Sarah laugh? (Genesis 18:13)
> Is anything too hard for the LORD? (Genesis 18:14)
> Hagar, where have you come from, and where are you going? (Genesis 16:8)
> What's the matter, Hagar? (Genesis 21:17)
> What is your name, Jacob? (Genesis 32:27)
> Why do you want to know my name? (Genesis 32:29)
> Moses, what is that in your hand? (Exodus 4:2)
> Moses, why are you crying out to me? (Exodus 14:15)
> Joshua, stand up! What are you doing down on your face? (Joshua 7:10)
> Job, where were you when I laid the earth's foundation? (Job 38:4)
> Elijah, what are you doing here? (1 Kings 19:9, 13)
> King of Judah, why do you worship gods who could not save their people? (2 Chronicles 25:15)
> You of little faith, why are you so afraid? (Matthew 8:26)
> Why are you thinking these things? (Mark 2:8)
> Why are you sleeping? (Luke 22:46)
> Why do you call me, "Lord, Lord," and do not do what I say? (Luke 6:46)
> Saul, Saul, why do you persecute me? (Acts 26:14)

God doesn't ask because He needs to know; He asks because He needs us to think about the answer. God asks great questions.

God Leads His People

When God brought Israel out of slavery, He started the general idea of the people of God who are owned and treasured by Him (Exodus 19:6). That phrase meant they were the people being led by God, unlike everyone else. After the ten plagues forced the Egyptians to let Israel go, God's leadership both amazed and terrified the people right from the start.

God explained the Israelites' next move, saying something like this: "Listen, Moses, I'm taking my people to the land of Canaan. Everyone normally takes this trip using a huge, well-traveled highway from Egypt to Canaan along the sea. It would take just a few weeks. We're not doing that. If my people faced battle as they passed through the Egyptian fortresses at the border, they would turn back (Exodus 13:17-18, GPT). So instead, I want you to start wandering aimlessly in the wilderness in the wrong direction from here to here, then over to there, and then finally you'll end up with your back against the Red Sea in the least strategic position conceivable. Pharaoh will conclude that you are hopelessly meandering around in the desert and strategically inept. He can't resist a ripe target like that. So he will rally his top charioteers and the special forces of one of the greatest militaries in the world and try to attack you" (Exodus 14:2-4, GPT).

If I had been Moses, about then I would have gingerly raised my hand and asked, "Umm, what part of this plan sounds like a good idea to you, O LORD? Could we reexamine the highway option?"

Amazingly, Exodus 14:4 just says, "So the Israelites did this." God didn't explain that He had a plan for them to cross the Red Sea on dry ground. Why, oh why doesn't God feel the need to clarify the most important parts of His plan? But no, He expects His people to take step-by-step directions, right up to the Red Sea and certain catastrophe—only later rescuing them in some unexpected way that only He could imagine. That's what it means to become the people of God, led by Him and by His unique reasoning.

God instructed His people to follow a cloud by day and a fire by night, and anyone who followed the cloud was part of the people of God, by definition:

> Whether the cloud stayed over the tabernacle for two days or a month or a year, the Israelites would remain in camp and not set out; but when it lifted, they would set out.
>
> NUMBERS 9:22

Ponder God's succinct plan for the wilderness: "Follow the cloud." Maybe some people thought, *We've camped here too long*. If they broke camp and left, they were out. Maybe someone else might think, *I'm not ready to move on*. If the cloud left and they stayed, they weren't the people of God either. The whole point was to follow the cloud.

Through that long wilderness time, God built into His people the habit of obedience. That's why it took forty years to go from Egypt to Israel instead of weeks or months. That's how long it takes for people to develop an immediate response of obedience without question. When they finally got ready to obey, they became fit to enter the land. When God said, "March around Jericho," they marched without much discussion.

God Does Not Change

I recognize that many people whom I respect believe that God no longer sends dreams and visions, no longer speaks, and no longer allows us to prophesy on His behalf. They say the Bible replaced all of that. I've heard them make some impressive biblical arguments.

I just disagree. I can't see how our receiving the Bible would change the habits of the God who inspired the Bible. As the prophet Amos said, "For the LORD is the one who shaped the mountains, stirs up the winds, and reveals his thoughts to mankind" (Amos 4:13, NLT). That's just who the Creator is. None of us would want to explain to God a theology that insists He can't or won't talk anytime He wants to. When I read the Bible, the simplest interpretation doesn't say that an end would come to God's normal pattern of talking with people. In fact, Peter quotes the prophet Joel to say that, as we approach the end times, maybe God will speak out even more:

> In the last days, God says, I will pour out my Spirit on all people. Your sons and daughters will prophesy, your young men will see visions, your old men will dream dreams. Even on my servants, both men and women, I will pour out my Spirit in those days, and they will prophesy.
>
> ACTS 2:17-18

He Still Speaks

Back in 1988, Rebecca and I spent our hours "studying" together down at the Kettle Restaurant's all-night breakfast buffet in College Station, Texas. Meanwhile, God got busy in West Africa informing the Yalunka people that they would soon have a chance to receive the gospel. The announcement came in the form of dreams to two old men. One man was called Vieux Sayon (Old Sayon), and the other was named

Manga Konbon (Chief Konbon). Both were old men when their dreams came, just as Joel said.

Much earlier in his life, Vieux Sayon had committed to follow Christ when the first missionaries came from the Christian and Missionary Alliance mission in the 1920s and 1930s. Sayon was the son of the first Yalunka Christian, Sergeant Bokari. He had been a good friend—some say the best friend—of the missionary who built a house and a church building in the village where we would later work and live.

People tell me that the whole village was considered Christian before the government changed in the 1960s and all the missionaries got kicked out. A time of persecution arose, and nearly everyone in town reverted to the religion they followed before, including Vieux Sayon and Manga Konbon. Manga Konbon became a well-known diviner who would tell people what sacrifices to offer to gain power from the spirits.

Then one night, Vieux Sayon had a dream. In his dream he saw American people soaring about the village with outstretched arms, like ominous human airplanes. He awoke with a start the next morning and told one of the few Christians left in the village about seeing dozens of Americans gliding about town.

"It was terrifying," he recounted.

Years later, his dream began to come true when Rebecca and I arrived to live in his village. But he told the same Christian man, "Just you wait! In my dream there were a bunch of them. *This* is just the beginning."

After a time, we began hosting dozens of short-term visitors. At one point, we had two houses and two huts lodging nearly a dozen Americans. Vieux Sayon nodded knowingly and said, "Yes, *this* is what I saw in my dream."

Manga Konbon had a different dream. One year the church invited all the non-Christian village leaders to join us to celebrate Christmas. He stood up and testified that everyone in the village should listen to the Christians because he had had a dream. In his dream, he looked up and saw two towns. One town was a place of great suffering. The other town reverberated with singing, music, and joy. Between the two towns he looked up, and there, high above, stood a glorious person. Manga Konbon called out to him: "Sir, I would like to go into the town with the music and celebration." The person sadly shook his head and said, "You can't, because you are not a Christian. You must go to the other town."

Did these dreams come from God? They both warned influential people about the future, to alert them that God intended to do something new among them—much like what happens in the Bible. I conclude from Scripture and from experiences like these that God really does still speak, just as He did with Abraham, Pharaoh, Joseph, Jacob, and others. God still lets people know what He's doing.

Although these newly perceived messages don't carry the same weight as the Word of God revealed in the Bible, we still ought to ponder them.

Do You Listen?

These two Yalunka men never did return to Christ, despite the warnings. The cares of the world and the pressures of the surrounding culture that followed the Quran were too much for them. These precious men had every opportunity, but they never chose to follow Jesus. They gradually grew frail and died while separated from Jesus and His gospel . . . which brings us to the next chapter.

God speaks to people to explain, warn, or question, but only certain people listen. The Bible says:

> The heavens declare the glory of God; the skies proclaim the work of his hands. Day after day they pour forth speech; night after night they reveal knowledge. They have no speech, they use no words; no sound is heard from them. Yet their voice goes out into all the earth, their words to the ends of the world.
>
> PSALM 19:1-4

We don't have to wonder if God still speaks. He reveals Himself to everyone, without exception. The difference between God's people and all other people scattered over the face of the earth is that, when God speaks, *His people listen.*

Discussion Questions

1. How important do you think it is to God that people know Him?
2. If you ever had a dream that you suspect came from God, what was it like? What did you learn from it?
3. Have you ever been praying and seen a mental image that seemed to communicate meaning to you? If so, what did you learn?
4. How does your experience of God leading you compare to how God works in the Bible?
5. Review the section about questions that God asks people. Which of God's questions is your favorite? Why?
6. What was God trying to make His people understand by asking that question?

CHAPTER 2

GOD'S PEOPLE LISTEN

For he is our God. We are the people he watches over, the flock under his care. If only you would listen to his voice today!

PSALM 95:7, NLT

AROUND THE SAME time that Vieux Sayon and Manga Konbon had dreams from God, I had a dream too. In my first year of college, I became certain that God was calling me to work in Guatemala. I had known missionaries who mainly worked in Guatemala, so it felt natural for me to gravitate to what I knew.

One night, I had a dream so real it felt like a vivid memory. I squatted by a fire, looked up, and saw several huts with domed grass roofs rising above me. I looked through the smoke of the fire across from me and saw an elderly woman squatting, staring back at me through the dancing flames and shimmering smoke. She spoke a sentence to me so clearly that I knew the words meant *something*. I found myself repeating them in my mind, desperately trying to memorize them, but she spoke in some other language.

At that moment I snapped awake, seized by a desire to write down each word, sure that someday I would hear them again and find out what they meant. As I went to brush my teeth, I repeated them to myself, but I felt the words slipping from my mind, like smoke gently rising out of my reach. I thought about the woman and the huts and realized that this dream didn't seem like Guatemala to me.

That day I told my friends about the dream. I remember telling one of them that I felt sure this dream would someday happen to me. I began to wonder what it meant about where I would go and what kind of work I would one day do.

Today, as a Bible translator, I cannot count how many hundreds of times I have squatted by a fire encircled by grass-roofed huts talking to an elderly woman while desperately struggling to jot down her words into a notebook so I could understand them. It wasn't just an average dream. It has since come true many times, and it started me on the road to considering that maybe God would send me to a rural village, a place just like the one we later lived in for twelve years. Maybe it meant that God would orient my calling around understanding language.

I could have awakened from that dream and thought, *Whoa, that was freaky!* then thought no more of it. But by being open to God's message to me, it made a difference.

God's people listen to God. In the Bible, He stands poised to explain, warn, and question; but the people of God also have a role to play. We must open our hearts to God's work.

When we ask and seek to know what He wants us to do, our God speaks to us. At the time of that dream, I had solidly in mind that I would work in Guatemala as a civil engineer.

God sent me that dream to shake up my expectations. He intended to warn me to watch carefully, not for my preconceived notions, but to remain open to other opportunities that He would soon show me.

That same year, I started taking a class called Perspectives on the World Christian Movement.[4] At the time, people said that only one missionary existed for every million Muslims in the world. I began to realize that God was directing me away from Guatemala and toward Muslims. But I still couldn't understand my dream. I didn't know of any Muslims living in villages, joyfully squatting by fires surrounded by mud huts with grass roofs. Not until much later did God show us that part. I heard about unreached peoples[5] for the first time when I took that class in 1987, and so I began to pray that God would prepare the hearts of an unreached people group ahead of me.

God uses people who listen. That's why God blessed Abraham. "I will do this," God said, "because Abraham *listened to me* and obeyed" (Genesis 26:5, NLT). God respects people who remain curious about Him, attentive to His Word, and open to learning about what He wants.

Ask for Guidance

Great leaders in the Bible set the example that God's people "inquire of the Lord" before almost every action. Consider Joshua, for instance. Whenever he received a battle plan from the Lord, the Israelites won. God told Joshua how to take Jericho with the simple instructions, "March around the city" (Joshua 6:3). Later, God explained in detail how to ambush the town of Ai.

But one day, a seemingly minor issue arose that tripped up

Joshua. The people of Gibeon arrived, asking to make a treaty. Really, they had pulled an elaborate trick so Joshua would think they had come from a faraway place and so make a treaty with them, contrary to God's direct orders. In the heat of the moment, Joshua felt qualified to make the decision himself. But the Bible calls him out: "The Israelites sampled their provisions but *did not inquire of the LORD*. Then Joshua made a treaty of peace with them" (Joshua 9:14-15).

Almost no issue is too small to ask God about and listen for His guidance, even when clear evidence sits right in front of you. God knows more than we do. God's servants learn to ask Him about pretty much everything!

King Saul learned too late that failing to inquire of God could be deadly:

> Saul died because he was unfaithful to the LORD;
> he did not keep the word of the LORD and even
> consulted a medium for guidance, and *did not inquire of the LORD*. So the LORD put him to death.
> 1 CHRONICLES 10:13-14

What kind of risks do we unknowingly take every day by not looking for guidance from God? Saul lost everything by not listening to God, even though his name itself comes from a root word that means "to ask or inquire."[6]

David became a better king than Saul by eagerly asking the Lord for guidance. David said, "Let us bring the ark of our God back to us, for we *did not inquire of it* during the reign of Saul" (1 Chronicles 13:3). David had a habit of inquiring of the Lord through an ephod, a decorative accessory a bit like a vest that a priest would wear over his other robes. The ephod's appearance and use might have differed over time (Exodus 28:4;

2 Samuel 6:14), but here I'm emphasizing how priests used it to ask God questions. By going to a priest wearing an ephod, David received direct guidance on how to gain victory in various battles (1 Samuel 23:9-13; 1 Samuel 30:7-8). Inquiring made the difference between good and bad leadership.

God expected David to consult Him and seek guidance about every detail, even how to transport the Ark itself. One time David failed to do this, putting the Ark on a new cart instead of using its poles, as God designed it. The ox pulling the cart stumbled, Uzzah instinctively reached out to steady the Ark, and instantly he fell dead. The Bible tells us that David became both "afraid" of God and "angry" that day (1 Chronicles 13:11-12). The king later explained, "It was because you, the Levites, did not bring it up the first time that the LORD our God broke out in anger against us. *We did not inquire of him* about how to do it in the prescribed way" (1 Chronicles 15:13). Inquiring and listening *matter*.

At his best, David frequently asked God for guidance. Nine times the Bible mentions that David inquired of the Lord.[7] Usually he asked something like, "Shall I go and attack the Philistines?" The Lord gave equally concise answers: "Go, I will deliver them into your hands" (1 Chronicles 14:10). That's pretty sweet. How could that kind of simple affirmation change your life?

Sometimes the guidance came with unexpected elaboration, as when the Lord said,

> Do not go straight up, but circle around behind them and attack them in front of the poplar trees. As soon as you hear the sound of marching in the tops of the poplar trees, move quickly.
>
> 2 SAMUEL 5:23-24

Even I could win with instructions like that! (The only question I have is what a poplar tree looks like.) David became a great king because he asked for and received great guidance—a simple recipe for leadership success in any age.

If we can get guidance from God, then why in the world would any of us do anything without it? Maybe we don't ask because we don't like what we might hear.

King Ahab handpicked four hundred "prophets" based on whether they told him what he wanted to hear. When Jehoshaphat, the ruler of the southern kingdom, came to visit, he felt disturbed by the four hundred "yes men" King Ahab had gathered. "Isn't there a prophet of the Lord still around here that we could ask?" he asked sheepishly (1 Kings 22:7, GPT). Ahab openly shared his feelings: "There is still one prophet through whom *we can inquire of the LORD*, but I hate him because he never prophesies anything good about me, but always bad" (1 Kings 22:8).

The evil Ahab felt free to say out loud what we sometimes privately think. God's guidance can inconvenience us. We would prefer to do what we want rather than hear God's world-shaking guidance.

Jeremiah had a word for those who try to serve God without asking Him for guidance: senseless. "The shepherds are senseless and *do not inquire of the LORD*; so they do not prosper and all their flock is scattered" (Jeremiah 10:21). Only a senseless leader would fail to ask God for direction.

But what if God sends me to some awful place? What if He tells me to do something I don't want to do? That's a real concern. Both have happened to me, and they're sure to happen to you, too, if you start asking for God's guidance. But just as Abraham, Saul, David, and Daniel discovered, the spiritual rewards for listening to God are immense; and greater still are the risks of living a life ignoring God. God's people learn to listen to Him.

Be a Good Priest

God didn't always just break open time and space to talk out loud to folks. He communicated in other ways too.

He built into the law of Moses, for example, a priestly system for receiving guidance. In Exodus 28, the Lord established the role of the priest and gave him some key jobs. The priest was to worship God in dignity and honor (Exodus 28:2). He would literally wear the names of the tribes of Israel on his shoulders as he entered the presence of God, bringing their names up to God as a prayerful reminder. He interceded for the people under his spiritual influence.

Priests made decisions that would promote justice among the people. They wore a gold plate on their forehead declaring them "HOLY TO THE LORD" so they could bring gifts from the people to God. A lot was at stake! The priest had to do the job properly "so that he will not die" (Exodus 28:35-36).

We don't talk much about another crucial job of the priest: He would wear a fancy cloth square on his chest containing special instruments to determine God's will and direction for the people *by casting lots*. This resembled the ephod that David used:

> Put the Urim and the Thummim in the breastpiece, so they may be over Aaron's heart whenever he enters the presence of the LORD. Thus Aaron will always bear the means of making decisions for the Israelites over his heart before the LORD.
>
> EXODUS 28:30

A mysterious element always accompanies hearing direction from God, but this elevates the process to a complete enigma. The priest had to somehow take objects of random chance, put them close to his heart, and then carry them into the presence of God—a strange process that yielded divine guidance.

One thing seems clear from all this: God wants to provide an everyday way for His people to know His will. The priests approached the presence of God holding the decision-making implements close to their hearts in the ephod. And God promised them: "There I will meet you and *speak to you*; there also I will meet with the Israelites" (Exodus 29:42-43).

Does it shock you to think that *you* have taken the place of both the Tabernacle and the priest? "Do you not know that your bodies are temples of the Holy Spirit?" (1 Corinthians 6:19). In the Kingdom, our bodies replace temples and physical places of worship. Peter says, "You are a chosen people, a royal priesthood, a holy nation, God's special possession" (1 Peter 2:9). John says that Jesus "has made us to be a kingdom and priests to serve his God and Father" (Revelation 1:6). When God looks at you, He sees the words "Holy to the Lord," just as if a shining gold plate were tied to your forehead.

Could this same God who met the priests be eager to meet you, even right now, also to "speak" to *you*?

Whose names do *you* bear on your shoulders, like a priest, into the presence of God? Whom do *you* represent before God, pleading that they, too, would come to be made holy by the blood of Jesus? How do *you* promote the justice of God in your community, as a priest would? And finally, do you know how to inquire of the Lord in our day?

A lot has changed from that time until now, but we are still

God's holy people. And people still need to know what God is saying. And yes, the process remains mysterious. That's okay. It's always been like that.

Hear from God in Worship

In addition to priests, God also speaks through prophets. "When there is a prophet among you, I, the LORD, reveal myself to them in visions, I speak to them in dreams" (Numbers 12:6).

During David's reign, the king started seeking God's will through prophets as well as priests. He asked Nathan about building a temple for God and eventually learned that his son, Solomon, would build the Temple (2 Samuel 7:2, 12-13). God provided prophets as another important way for people to hear from God.

While priests received guidance from God by casting lots with an ephod, prophets approached God in personal worship. Groups of prophets played tambourines, flutes, and harps while proclaiming the word of the Lord (1 Samuel 10:5; 1 Chronicles 25:1).

One day when Jehoshaphat the king of Judah had joined the king of Israel to fight against Moab, the Israelite army swung all the way around in a surprise attack from the desert, south of the Dead Sea, and ran completely out of water. After they exhausted their own ideas, they asked around, found Elisha, and petitioned him to ask God what to do.

"Bring me someone who can play the harp," Elisha replied. "While the harp was being played, the power of the LORD came upon Elisha, and he said, 'This is what the LORD says: This dry valley will be filled with pools of water!'" (2 Kings 3:15-16, NLT).

These prophets received the Word while worshiping. If you

wanted to hear from God in volume, you'd seek out an expert prophet, like Elisha or Jeremiah.

Jeremiah's Disconcerting History

As a Bible translator, I loved translating the book of Jeremiah; but something about it troubled me. Through each of his fifty-two chapters, almost no one ever listened to Jeremiah except Baruch. Nearly everyone else ignored him, spoke out against him, or even cut up and burned his writings.

Meanwhile, poor Jeremiah faithfully proclaimed the Word to reluctant ears. I can see why they eventually locked him up! The way I understand the text, he went door-to-door among the ambassadors' residences, proclaiming the word of the Lord (which is why it says that God called him to be a "prophet to the nations" in Jeremiah 1:5).

Imagine the shock as officials answered the door at each embassy:

> *Knock, knock*
> *Official:* Who is it?
> *Jeremiah:* It's the prophet of the Lord. I have the cup of God's wrath.
> *Official:* We don't want any.
> *Jeremiah:* "Drink, get drunk and vomit, and fall to rise no more because of the sword I will send among you. . . . You must drink it!" (Jeremiah 25:27-28).

That's hard core.

Another time Jeremiah went around from ambassador to ambassador, making a nuisance of himself while wearing a yoke. They would yank open the door, only to see the prophet with a wooden rod over his shoulders, hung with straps. Eventually, he took his message right to King Zedekiah: "Bow your neck under the yoke of the king of Babylon" (Jeremiah 27:12).

One day, as Jeremiah prophesied his message of defeat in the Temple, a false prophet ripped the yoke off his shoulders in frustration and broke it. Soon afterward, God gave Jeremiah another message: "You have broken a wooden yoke, but in its place you will get a yoke of iron" (Jeremiah 28:13).

Jeremiah so disrupted the politics of the day and created such a shock to the masses that the king felt he had to stop him. After all, war had broken out with Babylon . . . and Jeremiah proclaimed that the people of Judah would *lose.* That's pretty much prophetic treason!

But no one could silence Jeremiah under any circumstances, even after they lowered the prophet into the ooze at the bottom of a deep, slimy pit. They eventually got so furious with his message that they brutally beat him and threw him into Jonathan's jailhouse, where he nearly starved to death.

As I translated the story, my eyes filled with sympathetic tears. I felt astounded and frankly discouraged. "Lord," I asked, "if Jeremiah really was proclaiming Your word, then how could You allow his work to fail? No one ever, *ever* listened to him!" Would God really send out His prophet to preach for decades, with absolutely no success until the day he died?

But I really had another worry: "Lord, are You the kind of God who might pour *my* whole life down a dark drain?"

As I reflected, however, I realized, *Here I am, in West Africa, on a team translating every word Jeremiah wrote from Hebrew into Yalunka.* Even if no one listened to Jeremiah in his lifetime, *we are listening!* In fact, his book has now been translated into over seven hundred of the largest languages in the world, covering 80 percent of the world's population—almost six billion people.[8] People all over the earth are still learning from Jeremiah 2,600 years later. Now from the afterlife, Jeremiah can at last clearly see the full scope of the power of the word of the Lord!

Standing in God's Council Meetings

While I translated, I learned valuable lessons from Jeremiah about how to listen. God explained through Jeremiah that receiving the word of the Lord is like attending a meeting. Apparently, Jeremiah developed a habit of sitting in on the "secret council meetings" of the Lord. That's why Jeremiah proclaimed truth while other prophets told lies.

"But which of them has stood in *the council* of the Lord to see or to hear his word? Who has listened and heard his word?" (Jeremiah 23:18). God used the same word again several verses later: "But if they had stood in *my council*, they would have proclaimed my words to my people and would have turned them from their evil ways" (Jeremiah 23:22). The word translated "council" in both verses means a secret consultation or board meeting.

One Hebrew dictionary calls it a "confidential conversation" or a "circle of confidants."[9] Jeremiah got to attend God's planning meetings! Would you like that from time to time in your own life?

One secret to hearing from God is to show up at God's meetings. And it's crucial! Learning to hear God makes all the difference in ministry effectiveness. Jeremiah could prophesy seven hundred years in advance that Jesus would establish the new covenant (Jeremiah 31:31). Meanwhile, the other prophets predicted victory for Judah only days before the Babylonians wiped out Jerusalem.

If we want to know God's plan, we must show up at His planning meetings. We must invest ample time in God's presence.

Give God Time to Speak

After the smoke had cleared from the destruction of Jerusalem, Jeremiah's life set another compelling standard for hearing from God. God's wrath over the sin of His people didn't end with the destruction of Jerusalem. Judah had become so unfaithful and its repentance so slight that another avoidable calamity struck.

The Babylon-appointed governor was assassinated by an enemy nation trying to take advantage of Israel's weakness. Terror struck the hearts of the last remaining survivors in Israel. If their previous rebellions against Babylon warranted the destruction of Jerusalem, what would Babylon do to avenge the assassination of its governor? Anxious whispers about fleeing to Egypt rippled through the scattered community.

The last leaders of the land gathered up all the people and called in Jeremiah, the one and only prophet left, and certainly the only one with a recent winning track record. They asked him, point-blank, "Pray that the Lord your God will tell us where we should go and what we should do" (Jeremiah 42:3).

A hint of skepticism must have shown on Jeremiah's weathered face because they felt compelled to swear: "May the Lord be a true and faithful witness against us if we do not act in accordance with everything the Lord your God sends you to tell us" (Jeremiah 42:5). Every head in the crowd nodded, every mouth murmured, "No, Jeremiah, we promise this time *for real.* We will *totally* do whatever you say. We have learned our lesson! No matter what, we will do it" (42:6, GPT).

It's easy to miss the meat of the life lesson from Jeremiah. We see it right there several verses after their request: "*Ten days later* the word of the LORD came to Jeremiah" (Jeremiah 42:7). God took ten whole days to give Jeremiah the word of the Lord!

This observation might give us a clue as to why we don't hear much from God. When did you or I last dedicate ten days to hear God's direction on a crucial question? I can't remember ever doing exactly that.

If we want to know God's plan for our lives, we need to show up at God's planning meetings. We will need to invest in our prayer times, with a pen and paper handy, asking God to show us what He wants to do with our lives. Fifteen minutes won't do the job if you want to hear from the Lord. We will have to dedicate more time than that to get reliable guidance.

Jesus and Jeremiah Agree

Jesus agrees with Jeremiah. He clearly told Peter that the apostle wouldn't make it through temptation without a greater investment in prayer:

> Then he came and found them sleeping. So he said to Simon Peter, "Are you sleeping? Aren't you strong enough to keep watch through *an hour* of prayer? Keep watch and pray so that you won't give in to temptation. The spirit is eager but the body is weak."
> MARK 14:37-38, GPT

Jesus recommended that His disciples stay spiritually solid by praying an hour during times of testing. Of course, we never know when that testing might come, so it's safest to keep vigilant most days. If Jesus urged Peter to pray an hour to overcome temptation, what would He recommend Peter invest during a time of seeking God's direction on some crucial decision?

Okay, You Asked for It

After ten days of seeking the word of the Lord, Jeremiah returned and gave the people God's answer, one of the only times in the whole book that Jeremiah foretold peace for Israel: "If you stay in this land, I will build you up and not tear you down . . . for I have relented concerning the disaster I have inflicted on you" (Jeremiah 42:10).

After forty-one miserable chapters of proclaiming utter ruin, Jeremiah finally proclaims peace . . . but only if the people stay in the land. He patiently explains in verse 17 that if they flee to Egypt, the last of the people will be crushed beyond recovery by "sword, famine and plague."

Without reflection, without the benefit of any time seeking God's guidance, in a complete knee-jerk reaction, the people shouted, "You are lying!" (Jeremiah 43:2). In the final tragic irony of Jeremiah's life, the people dragged him down to Egypt, along with the rest of the remaining survivors. He apparently lived out the remainder of his days proclaiming doom in Egypt.

That's where Jeremiah's story ends. But as we look back over his prophetic words, we can see several nuggets of gold about hearing from God.

Jeremiah's Principles for Hearing God

Jeremiah tells us that when God opens His plans to you, you will know it. "'Is not my word like fire,' declares the LORD, 'and like a hammer that breaks a rock in pieces?'" (Jeremiah 23:29). You will know God's word when you hear it because it rages like a blazing fire and smashes like a sledgehammer.

God's words will obliterate your own goals in life and explode your well-organized schedule. They will lay claim to your life purpose, just like the words of my calling described at the beginning of this book: "While you still can!" I never recovered from the ringing blow of that hammer.

Second, Jeremiah warns us to watch out for prophets who tell us only what we want to hear. It is the exception, not the rule, that the word of the Lord will tell you, "Hey, keep doing what you want to do!" Jeremiah once explained this principle to a false prophet:

> From early times the prophets who preceded you and me have prophesied war, disaster and plague against many countries and great kingdoms. But the prophet who prophesies peace will be recognized as one truly sent by the LORD only if his prediction comes true.
> JEREMIAH 28:8-9

False prophecy most often falsely affirms our own desires: "'Peace, peace,' they say, when there is no peace" (Jeremiah 8:11). You can take it from Jeremiah that when you think you hear the word of the Lord, but it simply affirms what you already wanted, test that idea with twice the amount of discernment. It probably isn't the word of the Lord. When you sense a correction from God, that word will more readily prove to be from God because He often speaks to correct us.

A third lesson from Jeremiah reminds us that while God may be invisible, He's not hiding and He's not silent. He will not withhold His plans from you if you seek Him! When Babylon carried off the people into slavery, God's word followed them even there. In chapter 29, God inspires Jeremiah to send a letter to the exiles in Babylon in which he explains that the exile will end "when seventy years are completed" (verse 10). Then he makes another point about how to hear from God:

> "For I know the plans I have for you," declares the LORD, "plans to prosper you and not to harm you, plans to give you hope and a future. Then you will call on me and come and pray to me, and I will listen to you. You will seek me and find me when you seek me with all your heart. I will be found by you."
>
> JEREMIAH 29:11-14

God will not conceal His plans from His people! But it takes more than a half-hearted effort to understand what He says. You must seek Him with all your heart.

Seven Lessons about Guidance

Consider briefly seven lessons I have learned from the prophets, including Jeremiah, that resonate with my own spiritual experience:

- God reveals guidance while we worship.
- God expects us to show up at His planning meetings and listen.

- God's Word burns like a fire and smashes like a hammer.
- God's Word more often corrects us than affirms what we want.
- Hearing the word requires a concentrated time investment.
- God does not hide His plans from His people.
- People who seek God with all their heart will find Him.

You might say to yourself, "Well, of course Jeremiah could receive the word of the Lord! After all, he's an Old Testament prophet! I'm just a normal person."

Now, wait a minute. Don't forget that you have promises from God that Jeremiah *didn't* have.

Listen to the Holy Spirit

You may not imagine yourself to be a modern-day Jeremiah, Ezekiel, or Isaiah. And it's true, you can't be like them. No, you are *greater* than them! Jesus said:

> I tell you the truth, of all who have ever lived, none is greater than John the Baptist. Yet even the least person in the Kingdom of Heaven is greater than he is! . . . For before John came, all the prophets and the law of Moses looked forward to this present time.
>
> MATTHEW 11:11, 13, NLT

So, here's the score:

Prophets → John the Baptist → You

How could Jesus so confidently make such a sweeping statement about you and me? Jesus knows all about our human weakness, but He also knows the power of the Spirit. Jesus knew that with God's Holy Spirit, even if I happened to be the "least person in the Kingdom," I still have an advantage over any Old Testament prophet because the Spirit talks to me.

Paul encouraged believers to eagerly desire that the Spirit would give us the ability to prophesy so we can strengthen, comfort, and edify the Church (1 Corinthians 14:1-5). Jesus explained the Spirit's role in our lives like this:

> When you are brought before synagogues, rulers and authorities, do not worry about how you will defend yourselves or what you will say, for *the Holy Spirit will teach you* at that time what you should say.
>
> LUKE 12:11-12

Not only will He tell us what to say, He will also reveal true guidance from Jesus:

> When he, the Spirit of truth, comes, *he will guide you into all the truth.* He will not speak on his own; he will speak only what he hears, and he will tell you what is yet to come. He will glorify me because it is from me that he will receive what he will make known to you.
>
> JOHN 16:13-14

Jesus says that the Spirit will talk to His followers in days "yet to come," like now. Those people in times "yet to come" include individuals in churches like yours and mine. John tells believers in the church that the Spirit will teach them too:

> You have received the Holy Spirit, and he lives within you, so you don't need anyone to teach you what is true. For the Spirit teaches you everything you need to know, and what he teaches is true—it is not a lie. So just as he has taught you, remain in fellowship with Christ.
>
> 1 JOHN 2:27, NLT

If God meant this for them, He means it for you and me too.

The Spirit Speaks to Us

The Spirit talks to people. He has a voice that people can quote, just like any other person:

- *The Spirit told* Philip, "Go to that chariot and stay near it." (Acts 8:29)
- *The Spirit said* to [Peter], "Simon, three men are looking for you." (Acts 10:19)
- *The Holy Spirit said,* "Set apart for me Barnabas and Saul." (Acts 13:2)
- *The Spirit of Jesus would not allow* them to [enter]. (Acts 16:7)
- *The Holy Spirit tells* me in city after city that jail and suffering lie ahead. (Acts 20:23, NLT)
- *The Holy Spirit says,* "In this way the Jewish leaders in Jerusalem will bind the owner of this belt." (Acts 21:11)

This same Holy Spirit still speaks to you and me.

Listen to Jesus' Voice

Jesus said that His followers know His voice, hear Him, and follow. Jesus called Himself our Good Shepherd: "His sheep follow him because they know his voice" (John 10:4). He even makes it personal: "My sheep listen to my voice; I know them, and they follow me" (John 10:27).

Can you hear His voice?

Eleven times in the Gospels Jesus challenged people to listen to Him with an extraordinary capability to hear. He said things like "Whoever has ears, let them hear" (Matthew 11:15). I assume that He wasn't talking to a crowd of people who lacked physical ears. He was telling them to listen with spiritual understanding of His words. This kind of hearing does not require physical ears, but it does require spiritual ones.

This kind of hearing means being spiritually perceptive enough to understand what Jesus is saying through the Spirit and how it applies to our lives, and then learning to have a heart that spurs us to obedient action.

Someone could argue that Jesus spoke only about listening to His teachings in Scripture and not about hearing His voice today. But in the book of Revelation the resurrected Jesus keeps challenging the Church, even from heaven, saying seven times to John: "Whoever has ears, let them hear what the Spirit says to the churches" (Revelation 2:7). When Jesus said it the seventh time, He made the whole idea seem like a sweeping promise for all people, everywhere, every day:

> Here I am! I stand at the door and knock. If anyone *hears my voice* and opens the door, I will come in and eat with that person, and they with me. . . . Whoever

> has ears, let them hear what the Spirit says to the churches.
>
> REVELATION 3:20, 22

Today, if you hear Jesus' voice, open the door!

An African Friend Who Heard Jesus

I knew a West African man who could hear Jesus. Pastor Paul worked as a rugged, part-time preacher and a full-time farmer. Every tendon on his lean back rippled as he worked, stretched taut from decades of laboring in the red, gravel-crusted earth with hand tools crafted at the local blacksmith's forge. He trudged unknown miles behind his plow, dragged through the soil by oxen he raised and trained himself. Paul was among my closest, most precious friends until the day he died, all too young.

Every year when Rebecca and I return to West Africa, I notice the ruins of Paul's round hut jutting out of the ground near the church as we saunter down to worship. I can still see the remnants of a narrow concrete slab we poured in front of his door to keep out the mud. The leftover ruins of his hut don't look like much today, but they seldom fail to bring tears to my eyes as I remember Paul. I recall the hours we spent lounging on wooden benches by the fire, our feet resting on the thin concrete slab, heads pitched back in easy laughter, our voices echoing carelessly up into the starry African sky.

Paul invested most every waking hour in the arduous work of coaxing food out of the red, rocky earth to feed his growing family. Every year it was the same: He would struggle to break open the sloped earth, bent for hours daily over a three-foot-long hoe. He would scatter the rice seed on the churned-up soil, then till the seed, working it down into a thin layer of dust. As the rains poured out grace on the fields, the rice would sprout, shoot up quickly, and then bend over under the heft of the chunky heads of grain.

That's when it always happened. Flocks of yellow weavers and fire-crowned bishops would dart and swoop down on their migration, stripping lengths of palm leaves to cleverly weave nests dangling like grassy pearls from every palm tree. Some would even entwine two twelve-foot-tall stalks of grass together at the top to have their nest sway gently in the breeze, dotting the tops of the endless oceans of grass rippling on the West African savannah.

Small but voracious, these birds could wipe out a harvest by their vast numbers and starve out Paul's family. So Paul and his children took turns for two months of every year to do "bird chasing." It was a simple matter of stoically sitting in the field and periodically rising to run about, waving their arms and shouting, "Yah! Yah!" when the birds targeted their precious crop. They spent most of their time scanning the fields, which gave Paul time to pray . . . and to listen.

One day, as Paul prayerfully stood vigil over the field, God broke His silence. "Go north to preach," God told him. As Paul dutifully scared off passing flocks of birds, those words gnawed at him all day long. Whole towns and regions just north of his field had never heard the message of Jesus. I don't know how Paul knew, but a certain point came when he understood beyond a shadow of a doubt that God had sent *him*. He was to travel to the largest northern Yalunka village, a place where no one had ever shared the gospel of Jesus, from Creation until that moment.

I wish I had asked him more questions about how it happened and what it felt like. How did he know? It's too late to find out now. But he told me it happened. A moment came when this honorable farmer lifted his eyes over his rice field, meticulously searching every section for the twitching movement of birds—and he found instead the will of God.

He told me one evening: "There are towns north of here that have never in the history of the world heard the good news about Jesus. God has now given me three purposes for my life, three legacies I will leave behind after I die: to build a brick house with a metal roof for my family; to plant fruit trees to leave food behind for my children; and to proclaim the gospel in those towns up north."

Not long afterward, he and a future pastor named Bokari set out on their bicycles on an evangelistic tour of villages until they finally arrived at the major village that God had put on Paul's heart. They approached the town chiefs and the local religious teacher. They explained their mission and the message of Jesus. The village leaders all listened intently.

When the time came for them to give an answer, the religious teacher of the village spoke clearly: "Here in our town, we want only one religion. We don't want Jesus' religion here." And so Paul and Bokari got back on their bicycles and headed home, dejected.

More than twenty years later, a small gathering of believers started meeting in that town. Someday I expect a thriving network of churches to spread all over that region. Paul and Bokari will forever hold the honor of being the first to obey Jesus' command in that place. That year, they claimed a place in church history.

Throughout eternity in heaven, when those who got saved from that town and region gather to tell the spiritual history of their region, the story will begin in a rice field lovingly scoured free of birds, and it will tell how God spoke to a pensive farmer as he prayerfully listened for direction.

In the church where pastor Paul preached for decades before his death, it became tradition to regularly read Hebrews 4. They punched home this one verse, over and over, for years and years: "Today, if you hear his voice, do not harden your hearts" (Hebrews 4:7). It's the word "Today" that hits home every time. I think that was their way of saying, "Listen, my fellow followers of Jesus. God's voice could break through the silence at any moment." *Today*, it could happen. You might hear God. At any moment, He could send you on your bicycle up north to preach the gospel.

Do you have ears to hear? And if you do hear Him, don't harden your heart like so many have done. Today, when you hear God's voice, be the kind of person who says, "Here I am, Lord, Your servant is listening."

Discussion Questions

1. About what kinds of things do you inquire of the Lord?
2. What have you not inquired about that you now intend to start asking?
3. How do you play a role like a priest for the people around you, helping them learn to receive guidance from God?
4. How much time should we realistically spend listening in the presence of God, like Jeremiah attending the Lord's council meetings?
5. How often do you sense the guidance of the Holy Spirit in your life? What is that like for you?
6. What would need to change in your life to have a heart that hears God?

PART 2

LEARNING TO WALK WITH GOD

CHAPTER 3

PROACTIVE DEVOTION

I will climb up to my watchtower and . . .
wait to see what the L*ORD* *says.*

HABAKKUK 2:1, NLT

A HAND-PAINTED SIGN posted beside a lonely stretch of African road provoked the most far-fetched plot twist in my life's story. Back then, road traffic only intermittently traversed the village where we eventually would choose to settle our family. Ladies could scatter their grain along the edges of the pavement of the highway to dry in the brutal sunlight. People could stand undisturbed in the roadway long enough to have a casual conversation, only periodically disrupted by a careening four-wheel-drive vehicle veering around the corner and swerving by in the other lane.

Occasionally, a massive market truck loaded twenty feet high or more would explode onto the scene of the peaceful town, scattering sheep and chickens while growling down the roadway, swaying heavily back and forth under the undulating influence of the shifting load.

No one could have imagined that one of these passing vehicles would permanently alter the lives of most everyone in town. And my whole world would never be the same.

A seasoned missionary named Kent had headed from the Forest Region of the country to the capital city—he thought, perhaps, for the last time. He was getting ready to leave. As he raced through the countryside, on the left he saw an unremarkable cluster of huts and a gravel-covered area clear of grass and trees, where cars could easily pull off the road. There, some brightly painted words caught his eye on a placard: *Foyer Chrétien* (Christian Household).

Kent's eyes locked onto the message as he whisked past. He must have pulled his foot off the accelerator to ponder for a moment as he coasted and mused, *Wait a minute, I thought this whole region was only Muslims. Who are these people announcing "Christian Household"?*

Most of us probably would have rolled on by for a second or two and then resumed our journey without thinking twice. But Kent felt overwhelmed by a sense that *something* divinely significant had just happened. He stopped and got out of his vehicle to ask about the sign. He soon discovered that a little group of Christians lived in the village—the only Yalunka Christians on our side of the border.

Kent could get only so far with hand gestures and soon realized that most villagers didn't speak much French. They spoke mostly Yalunka.

All the way back to the city, he couldn't shake the notion that he *had* to go back to that little town. But how could he communicate with the villagers? That line of reasoning is what brought the ministry of Pioneer Bible Translators from that area into the picture. They had a team of people who spoke fluently a closely related language.

Two of our colleagues agreed to go back with Kent to help him communicate with the Yalunka people, helping him explore his inexplicable curiosity about that sign. Somehow, God had impressed upon Kent's soul this thought: *This is a watershed moment.* Together they made the arduous eight-or-nine-hour journey back to the village for a visit.

All that time, Rebecca and I remained blissfully unaware, living in France to learn French as part of our preparation to work in West Africa. We had prayed for years that God would prepare an unreached people group for us. In France, we passed our time joyfully riding bicycles from bakery to bakery, checking out castles, and learning how to speak French in between bites of Camembert cheese and *pain au chocolat*—by far the cushiest assignment we would ever undertake in the name of Jesus.

Meanwhile, back in West Africa, Kent and my two teammates went together to see if they could communicate with this lone church among the Yalunka people. They first approached a pastor in the nearby town. The pastor sent his son ahead of them to the village to inform the church that they would soon host a small troop of foreigners.

When that young man returned, he announced that he had found the tiny Yalunka church just finishing up a forty-day fasting and prayer time in which they had asked God to send someone to help them evangelize their own people. It quickly became clear that Kent's feeling that God wanted them there exactly correlated with the church's fasting and prayer for help. God had orchestrated the whole situation.

When the missionary visitors met with the people in the

church, everyone felt awestruck at how God was working a miraculous answer to their prayers. The missionaries asked the local church to start praying for a couple named Greg and Rebecca Pruett to come there. Everyone could sense God's leading in the situation, and they all just *knew* that God was calling us to go there—everyone, that is, except us. We knew nothing of the whole incredible story. For us, it unfolded like a life-altering spiritual ambush.

Our leader and mentor flew from West Africa to France to meet us at a train station in Paris. He sat us down over ham baguette sandwiches on a chilly park bench and told us the news that God had prepared a place for us.

I felt taken aback. This wasn't my plan! But as I think back on it, I still can't keep from feeling profoundly moved by God's unparalleled grace. For several years we had fervently prayed that God might prepare a place where we could serve Him among the least reached peoples of the world. All the while, this solitary, small church had cried out to God as well, asking Him to send someone to help them. They didn't know us, but they had prayed for us, supported us, and ultimately (spiritually speaking) hijacked our lives through the power of their prayers until we made our home with them for twelve and a half years. God was behind it all, just out of sight, orchestrating the whole scene like a director guiding a theatrical performance. God brought so many disparate forces together to make the Yalunka Bible translation project possible!

What if Kent had not lived a life sensitive to the leading of the Spirit? What if Rebecca and I had not prayed for years for God to prepare the way for us? What if the Yalunka people had not fasted and prayed for help? We don't know. But what we do know is that when all of these people *were* seeking God, He did not hide from us. He moved in power to guide us all into His divinely chosen path, at His appointed time.

The Yalunka people now have a Bible. They now have the beginnings of a church movement in several villages. They even have a vision to reach out to the surrounding unreached peoples. But all of that started with a group of praying villagers and a man named Kent driving down the road with a heart well-prepared to hear from God.

That's what the next nine chapters are about: spiritual preparation. How can we cultivate our hearts to have that extraordinary hearing? To hear God, we must first draw near and walk with Him.

Walk with God to Hear God

Walking with God is no accident. Think about men and women in the Bible who had great faith. What about them made them become prophets? We get the impression they just walked along, minding their own business, when *bam*! God spoke to them:

God: Noah!
Noah: What? Who is this?
God: It's the Lord.
Noah: Who is this, really?

It didn't happen like that. Noah already knew God. The story says, "Noah was a righteous man, blameless among the people of his time, and he walked faithfully with God" (Genesis 6:9). That last phrase could be rendered literally from the original language as "Noah walked with God."

So how does a person walk with God?

We have other inspiring examples. Enoch walked with God (Genesis 5:24). David was a man after God's own heart (1 Samuel 13:14). Joshua would not leave God's presence in the tent of meeting (Exodus 33:11). The boy Samuel slept near the Ark of God (1 Samuel 3:3). Simeon and Anna regularly worshiped in the Temple (Luke 2:27, 37). These people didn't hear a voice and *then* approach God. No, first they approached God, and only then did they hear His voice: "God is light . . . If we walk in the light, as he is in the light, we have fellowship with one another" (1 John 1:5, 7).

We have fellowship with God when we walk in the light with Him.

He won't shout at us from across a crowded room. Normally, He won't hunt us down, tackle us, and explain His will. No, you and I need to develop a pattern of proactively seeking God in our daily lives. We never know when God will call us to fulfill His plan—like Kent driving down that lonely road in Africa. We need to wait for the Lord in readiness. As the Word explains, "The Lord looks down from heaven on all mankind to see if there are any who understand, any who seek God" (Psalm 14:2). He searches the earth even now.

PROACTIVE Devotional Life

I use a memory device to help me build every habit I need to walk closely with God and hear Him speak. Each of the next nine chapters will unfold a crucial way to move your relationship with Him forward:

Pattern	Chapter 4
Read	Chapter 5
Obey	Chapter 6
Adore	Chapter 7
Confess	Chapter 8
Thank	Chapter 9
Intercede	Chapter 10
Vanquish	Chapter 11
Extreme Prayer	Chapter 12

I based the memory device PROACTIVE on the acronym ACTS first used in the 1800s. I revised and expanded ACTS to ACTIVE in my first book, *Extreme Prayer*. All but one of the letters in ACTIVE is based on the prayer Jesus taught His followers in Matthew 6:9-13.

Adoration	Our Father in heaven, hallowed be your name. (verse 9)
Confession	And forgive us our debts, as we also have forgiven our debtors. (verse 12)
Thanksgiving	
Intercession	Give us today our daily bread. (verse 11)
Vanquishing Satan	And lead us not into temptation, but deliver us from the evil one. (verse 13)
Extreme Prayer	Your kingdom come, your will be done, on earth as it is in heaven. (verse 10)

Extreme prayer refers to praying the impossible, Kingdom-oriented prayers that Jesus promised to answer with unlimited power. Almost all the elements of an ACTIVE prayer life are there in the prayer Jesus taught, just in a different order.

Ironically, the only missing letter is the *T* for thanksgiving. I doubt anyone would argue that the Bible teaches us to skip gratitude! In fact, adoration and thanksgiving are closely linked, which means the entire ACTIVE memory device has been built on the firm foundation of Jesus' model prayer.

But there's more to a balanced spiritual walk with God than prayer. We need constant input from Scripture to learn how to hear from God. That's why I put the three letters PRO on the front of ACTIVE, to highlight that we need to **P**attern our lives with special times of spiritual nourishment that include **R**eading and **O**beying Scripture. All these PROACTIVE elements, working together, provide the foundation for getting ready for extraordinary hearing, the ability to receive reliable guidance from God.

Tilling the Soil

Having a PROACTIVE devotional lifestyle tills the soil of your heart. Do you remember the parable of the sower? A farmer goes out and tosses seeds that fall on all types of soil. The soil represents the hearts of people. The story describes three kinds of bad soil but only one type of good soil, ready to receive the message of God and bear eternal fruit.

Jesus makes sure His followers realize that the message of the story focuses on the condition of the soil. If you don't prepare your heart as fertile soil, you run the risk of misunderstanding or not receiving any message that God sends you. In the passage, Jesus quotes Isaiah: "You listen and you listen, but you won't ever catch on. You look and you look, but you won't really see" (Matthew 13:14, GPT).

Isaiah 6:9-10, quoted here, says that people's hearts are too "calloused." The word translated "calloused" refers to growing fat or thickening, which hits a little too close to home for me. The idea seems to be that people can live such a prosperous life that their heart gets gristled up with a hardened layer of fat. Jesus longs for people to be ready to "hear with their ears, understand with their hearts and turn" so He can heal them (Matthew 13:15).

Jesus ends the parable by saying, "Whoever has ears, let them hear" (Matthew 13:9). He's telling us to proactively prepare the soil of our souls so that, when God scatters His messages on us, our hearts will be like well-watered, softened soil, warm and ready for seeds to sprout. Whether He sends us His messages through the written Word, preaching, dreams, visions, or by directly speaking into our minds, we will be ready. He controls the messages; we control our daily spiritual activities that keep the soil of our hearts ready.

Preparing our hearts can change everything, as in the story at the beginning of this chapter.

Who Posted That Sign?

Who posted that "Christian Household" sign along the road in the first place? I wouldn't find out until many years later.

In 1997, we had prayed for a gifted Yalunka translator who could create the first draft of Scriptures, preferably someone smart and well-educated with a lot of availability. My close friend Pastor Paul brought to our door a young man named Dansa, his nephew.

Dansa was so clever that he greatly accelerated the whole translation project. For more than twenty-five years, Dansa worked first as a translator, then as a church planter, then again as a translation facilitator on a project for a neighboring language. He regularly rode his motorcycle to distant villages to preach. He's a Yalunka missionary.

One day, Dansa told me a story. Years ago, he said, when he was a student, he came home to his village to take a break from his studies. He noticed that the taxi drivers kept pulling over at the cluster of huts where his Christian family lived—including Pastor Daniel, the revered, elderly Yalunka pastor. They kept stopping to ask for water for their religious cleansing rituals before their prayers.

It didn't seem fitting to Dansa that the esteemed Pastor Daniel should have to spend his days providing water for prayer rituals for followers of a different religion. So out of concern for Pastor Daniel, Dansa put up a sign to explain the situation. It read in simple French, "Christian Household."

Even though this young student came from a family surrounded by oppressive religious influences of a different world religion, he didn't bow to pressure. He took a public stand for his faith and put that sign out there for all to see. Then he returned to the capital city to continue his studies.

God had set the stage for the whole drama to unfold when Kent would see that sign.

Dansa didn't know that God used his sign to flip my world upside down and start a translation project that would later provide much of the purpose of his own life. He just determined to be faithful. Before I prayed, before the village church prayed, before Kent drove by, a young student wrote a sign that started everything. God looked down on Dansa's faithfulness and began to work.

"Small" acts of faith don't exist, because even small acts of faith attract the power of an omnipotent God.

What might happen in your life when you prepare your soul to hear from God?

Discussion Questions

1. Think of a time when God interrupted your daily life to start something new. How did it happen?
2. How do you think your life might change if you set up a pattern of reading Scripture and praying every day?
3. What do you think is the hardest part of continuing to read Scripture and pray every day?
4. What have you learned that has helped you stay consistent with your Scripture reading and prayer?
5. How will you strengthen your devotional life this week to better hear from God?

CHAPTER 4

PATTERN

And your ears shall hear a word behind you, saying, "This is the way, walk in it," when you turn to the right or when you turn to the left.

ISAIAH 30:21, ESV

P R O A C T I V E
a
t
t
e
r
n

I GET ANGRY and upset if someone moves my deodorant. Don't judge me; I have my reasons.

I travel a lot. Ordinarily, my traveling runs smoothly because I have patterns in place. I keep one set of deodorant and toothpaste in my travel kit and another set on the counter in the bathroom. When I travel, I simply plop my travel kit into the suitcase without thinking about it. Then I don't stink. Everyone wins.

But at the beginning of every year, my system fails. I travel with my wife to West Africa, where she upends my systems. She feels strongly that we should obey the security rules and pack all our liquids in a separate Ziploc bag. That tiny little change blows up my systems. Without fail, I take my next trip without deodorant or toothpaste. Everyone suffers.

This has happened for years. Why can't I just consciously remember the problem and fix it? Because in my life, everything hinges on subconscious patterns.

You Have Patterns Too

Your life depends on patterns too. Do you remember learning how to change lanes in your car? The first time was tough. "Check your blind spot!" shouted your father. Then, "Signal with your blinker!" came another tersely barked command. "Don't weave when you check your blind spot!"

You endured a lot of drama that first time or two. Maybe for some of us, it took twenty or even fifty times to get the hang of it.

But when did you last think about checking your blind spot or using your turn signal? All of that has become a subconscious pattern built right into the chemicals in your brain. That whole series of actions happens flawlessly without a single conscious thought.

In fact, you can drive long distances without ever consciously thinking about it. I know because once a month I get in my car, intending to visit my allergist for my regular shot. But sometimes, the next thing I know, I'm at work, sitting in front of my computer. I have no recollection of driving to the wrong location, walking into my office, or booting up my computer. Turning down the road to my office on my way to the allergist's triggers a deeply ingrained series of habits. My subconscious takes over and executes the pattern it knows so well. And there I am, at the wrong place, wondering what happened.

Is it just me, or have you been there too? We humans are born with an automatic pilot feature, functioning on subconscious patterns.

The Spiritual Significance of Life Patterns

I first began to reflect on the spiritual significance of such patterns while reading a popular business book on habits. The author claimed that habit loops shape much of our lives:

> Habits, scientists say, emerge because the brain is constantly looking for ways to save effort. Left to its own devices, the brain will try to make almost any routine into a habit, because habits allow our minds to ramp down more often.[10]

Anything we do more than once can become a habit, especially if the brain can perceive a reward from it—like eating chips, brushing your teeth, or praying before bed. This author explains that habits form when three elements create a loop: (1) a cue, (2) a routine, and (3) a reward. These habit loops can form at any point in the day where we have a "cue," such as when we get up in the morning, when we arrive at work, when we come home, or when we go to bed.

I often hear people complain that they have never spent consistent time praying. With a guilt-ridden grimace, they explain that they just get busy and forget. I doubt that consciously trying hard to remember will ever solve the problem. The minute you get stressed, your discipline will lapse.

Instead, pick a cue that happens every day and build a formidable habit around it. Create a tenacious pattern that forms an impenetrable bastion of Scripture reading and prayer, triggered by that moment of the day.

Have you ever had a bad habit that felt impossible to break? Good habits can become just as powerful as bad habits.

While you can't have your devotional time subconsciously, the *decision* to pray can become a subconscious, ingrained habit. What if prayer became an immutable pattern woven into the fabric of your day?

Getting Started

Let's start by picking a specific time of day. For me, it's the morning. Every time I wake up, *boom*, that's the cue for my morning routine. So far, I have awakened every morning of my life, so this thing is consistent.

As soon as I wake up and my feet hit the floor, I am already on my way to do my routine. I weigh myself, make a pot of coffee for the family, and then, automatically, I head to a particular chair in my living room. Next to that chair, I have collected everything I need for my prayer time: my Bible, my prayer list, my pen, and my reading glasses (I'm over fifty now).

On the shelf behind me, I have Hebrew and Greek Bibles for when my inner Scripture nerd seizes the upper hand. I keep my phone charged and nearby for when I need my apps to research Greek or Hebrew words or maps for locations mentioned in the Bible. It's all right there so that my Scripture reading can be as productive as possible.

Starting the pattern was simple. I consciously decided to do the routine one morning. Then, I did it again the next morning. Then, I kept working at repeating it. I liked how it felt to be with the Lord, taking time to listen. I liked growing in personal holiness. It felt restful and transformative. I received direction from God. The pleasure of God's presence reinforced the habit loop. Then before I knew it, I was hooked. My mind had created a habit loop that now repeats every day.

A cue: Getting up in the morning.
A routine: Reading Scripture and praying in the same chair.
A reward: Inner peace and hearing marching orders from God.

Then one day, my wife rearranged the furniture. Argh! No worries, I just picked another chair, moved all my stuff, and reestablished the pattern.

But how can I keep the habit going when I travel? Most hotel rooms have a chair. When I walk into the hotel room, I put my computer bag down next to that chair. The Bible, the pen, and the prayer request list all wait in the bag. *Boom!* I'm back in business with my system.

Doesn't it get boring to follow the same pattern every day? No, it doesn't. That's my personality type. But if it did, not to worry, because I have a second possible routine that I also can cue.

Instead of praying through my prayer list, I read Scripture in the chair and then go for a run. As I run, I internally pray through my workplace. I picture mentally going from office to office, praying for each of my coworkers in the order that I come across them in the building. Then, as I physically run through the neighborhood, I mentally run around the entire world. I run through West Africa, North Africa, East Africa, up to Italy, across to Ukraine, the Caucasus, and on and on, praying for the people I know and influence in each of those places.

I never, *ever* make it all the way through the whole world. I get partway through, and then my mind wanders. Some issue suddenly pops into my mind that affects someone for whom I'm praying. While my mind wanders and my body runs, God puts good ideas into my head. I get solutions to problems, ideas for sermons, and entire emails. I grab my phone and tell Siri to take a note for me while I huff and puff through the idea.

I have built several prayerful patterns to choose from, and when I get up in the morning, I activate one of those habits. I can even develop a different spiritual pattern for each of the transition points in my day.

Transition Point Habits

At the beginning of 2020, we started a fundraising campaign for Pioneer Bible Translators. We established a target of $8 million. Unfortunately, we started just a few weeks before the COVID-19 lockdowns began.

The first phase went slowly all through the pandemic. But we stuck with it. One day I visited one of our donors to ask him to participate in the campaign. He did, but he helped us even more with a story he told.

Back in his younger days, he needed a loan to start his business. At that early stage of his illustrious career, the bank likely would not look with favor upon his financial situation. He said he went down to the bank on a Sunday and marched around it seven times, praying.

The bank granted the loan.

That next week, Rich, the chief development officer

overseeing our campaign, and I decided to walk around the property of our International Service Center in Dallas. We stopped and prayed at the site of the future facility expansion included in the campaign. We invited others to join us. A spiritual habit was born.

These days, regularly during lunch, a few of us go out and march around the property and pray. It makes for a pleasant fifteen-minute activity that gets our blood circulating and gives us a chance to spend time together. The campaign really picked up momentum by the third week of our marching around. It wouldn't surprise me if we keep doing it once the campaign ends.

A good spiritual habit should be sustainable, life giving, and a source of joy—not guilt inducing, something you wish you could "get motivated" to do. Building spiritual habits shouldn't feel overwhelming. Start with one good habit. Repeat it until it gets ingrained. Then start another. You need only a trigger for the habit, like lunchtime, waking up, or going to bed—the transition points of your day. As John Maxwell said, "You cannot change your life until you change something you do every day."[11]

What Patterns Mark Your Life?

So what patterns are you building into your life?

Do you need help? Some people use reading plans on the YouVersion app or Bible Gateway. Others enjoy watching the Bible Project videos. I listen to the Lectio 365 app for morning and night devotionals. I have a friend who runs a website called JourneyEveryDay.com. Just try *something.*

We talk about prayer as a spiritual discipline, like running for exercise. So when we hear the preacher quote

1 Thessalonians 5:17, "pray without ceasing" (ESV), we immediately get hit with a wave of exhaustion, as if he had said, "run without ceasing." We think, *Pastor, I know I should, but when I get home from work, I'm just so worn out. I don't have the energy. I'm not really good at it. I'm not disciplined enough. I know I should. But when I wake up in the morning, I'm so busy. I just don't have enough time.* We react to praying just like we do to running.

But what if we plucked it out of that category and slyly shifted it over into the same category as eating? Now that's more like it: "Brothers and sisters, *eat* without ceasing." Finally, something I'm qualified to do!

We would say things like, "Lately, I've been over-praying. I've been stress-praying a lot. I don't know what's happening to me. I lose control, and I just go on a binge. I've been snacking a lot in between prayer times—I just get so hungry! The other night at church we had an all-you-can-pray buffet."

See, we've just put prayer in the wrong category. Prayer sustains the body of Christ, like food does. Jesus feeds His people and His church *through prayer*.

We all know that eating becomes a well-ingrained habit for us. We get up in the morning, hear a little growl from the stomach, and know it's time for breakfast. Around the middle of the day, we get a little empty as the clock hits noon, and we know it's time for lunch. In the evening, no one tells us, "Oh, hey, by the way, there's this thing called dinner that I want to remind you about. You should have the discipline to try it." No, we feel keen to plunge into a good meal every evening. We don't skip many meals if we can help it! Eating quickly becomes a pattern of sustenance. We don't eat just once and stop. No! Morning, noon, and night, we eat. Our bodies need it. Eventually we come to crave it.

Don't starve yourself spiritually! Put Scripture and prayer into your day, just as you do eating. Daniel did: "He went home and knelt down as usual in his upstairs room, with its windows open toward Jerusalem. He prayed three times a day, just as he had always done, giving thanks to his God" (Daniel 6:10, NLT). That's a pattern.

What routine will be the most powerful for spiritual growth in your life?

Take a moment and look at the table in the discussion section below. Get creative. Sketch in the table some possible habits to build. When building your PROACTIVE devotional life, remember that the *P* stands for weaving spiritual *patterns* into your life that till the soil of your heart, preparing your soul to hear from God.

Discussion Questions

Take some time to think about the transition points of your day:

Transition Points	Spiritual Habits
Waking up	
Driving to work or school	
Arriving at work or school	
Lunchtime	

Transition Points	Spiritual Habits
Driving home	
Arriving at home	
Evening reminder alarm	
Before going to bed	
Lying down to sleep	

1. What is the first, highest priority spiritual habit you need to start?
2. Into what part of the day would it most naturally fit?
3. What might be a second or third spiritual habit you could start after that?
4. When would be the best part of the day to read Scripture, and where would be the most convenient place for you to build that routine?
5. How do you think building spiritual patterns into your day might impact how you hear from God?

CHAPTER 5

READ

Son of man, let all my words sink deep into your own heart first. Listen to them carefully for yourself.

EZEKIEL 3:10, NLT

P R O A C T I V E
e
a
d

I LOVED EATING supper with my family when I was little. Mom would cook a phenomenal meal. We would tell stories, crack jokes, and laugh until we cried and artificially sweetened tea ran out of our noses. It was all very old-school family back then. I treasure the memories.

It didn't happen every night, but often Mom would do the best thing of all. She would turn to me and say, "Greg, go get my Bible." I was tiny. I remember my mother like a titan towering over me. With my short attention span at the time, sending me in search of an object seemed no more reliable than trusting a dog to fetch you a snack from your refrigerator. But I never remember having to think hard about where to find Mom's Bible. She had patterns in her life too. I could race right to her Bible and sprint back in a flash.

One particular night shaped me forever. She couldn't have known what would happen. She had just shared a Scripture with the family: Isaiah 40. She'd zeroed in on verses 30 and 31 from the old Good News Bible featuring those disturbing stick-figure illustrations and a gold cover with vertical black lines streaking the bottom half. That night we memorized: "Even those who are young grow weak; young men can fall exhausted. But those who trust in the LORD for help will find their strength renewed. They will rise on wings like eagles; they will run and not get weary; they will walk and not grow weak." That verse carried me through many hard situations.

In the seventh grade I delivered newspapers. You remember newspapers, don't you? They were like the internet, except people rolled them up and threw them on your lawn.

I remember trying to carry one hundred newspapers on my bicycle through our neighborhood. I would piston those pedals up and down to a state of exhaustion. As my energy faded, I got to the place where even one more rotation of the pedals felt unthinkable. Looking up the hill and into the stiff winter wind, I would wink away drops from the corner of my eye—part sweat, part tears. And then the words would start involuntarily.

"Even those who are young grow weak." The truth would strike a chord resonating in my gut. "Young men can fall exhausted." By now I barely pedaled enough to keep the bike upright. "But those who trust in the LORD for help . . ." Suddenly a tiny spark of trust glowed in my heart as my soul began to seek to trust the Lord. An inkling of power tingled in my leg muscles. ". . . Will find their strength renewed." I stood up on my bike, pedaling harder, until the whole bike slanted way out from side to side with the effort of hard pumping. "They will rise on wings like eagles." Involuntary grunts of effort accompanied each stroke and an inexplicable surge of energy filled me.

I recited the rest of the verse to a backdrop of houses whipping past as I raced along, chucking papers right and left. Somehow, when my mother scattered this good seed of God's Word on my heart, those two verses thrust a profound root deep into my soul. I came to know and experience God and His power.

I could never repay my mother for the gift of her passion for Scripture. I saw her reading it in the mornings and late at night. Her dozens of Bibles tended to grow thicker with time as the pages crinkled with use. Until she shared Scripture with me, it mystified me. What could be so crucial about ancient words? But when I engaged Scripture for myself, I found not words but the Author behind the words, right there waiting for me. He made sure I never stayed the same.

Read the Bible to Know God

Once you establish patterns in your life for when and how your spiritual growth will take place (discussed in chapter 4), make Scripture reading your first priority. It's the most foundational part of tilling the soil of your heart in preparation for extraordinary hearing.

But the Scripture reading we need doesn't focus on *learning information* about the Bible. We don't emphasize knowing *about* God but knowing *God*. A friend of mine, Rich Sheeley, helped me understand the importance of reading Scripture to know the Author.

Rich bought a journaling Bible with wide space for writing

in the margins and started jotting down reactions to the verses, as though he were answering emails from God. He told me that he had always had trouble developing a strong habit of reading Scripture *so long as he read for knowledge.* After a certain time, he felt as though he knew most of what he needed to know. So it became less of a priority. Only when he saw reading Scripture as an opportunity to interact with the Author of Scripture did he become more passionate again about reading the Bible.

It's like the resurrected Jesus said in the book of Revelation: "Look! I stand at the door and knock. If you hear my voice and open the door, I will come in, and we will share a meal together as friends" (Revelation 3:20, NLT).

When I get out of bed every morning to start my routine of Scripture reading, I sense a subtle, faint knocking just out of range of my senses. The first step in reading the Bible is to start by opening the door. A universe of difference exists between reading the Bible with the door open and reading with the door closed. With my heart open, reading can become a precious conversation. Or it can just be reading. We decide. Every day, *we* open the door!

Tomorrow morning, sit down in a chair with your Bible. Dwell on the fact that the resurrected Jesus remains ever-present. Imagine what He might look like, maybe above you, looking down patiently, or maybe seated on a nearby chair. Picture in your mind a door closed between you. Then decide in your mind to reach out, turn the knob, and open the door. While you read the Word, keep that assurance of Jesus' presence firmly in mind, since He said He would be there. Ask Him questions about what you read. Wait to see how He will use the words in a special way to help change you.

He *will* use His Word:

> Come to me with your ears wide open. Listen, and you will find life. . . . The rain and snow come down from the heavens. . . . They cause the grain to grow. . . . It is the same with my word. I send it out, and it always produces fruit. It will accomplish all I want it to.
>
> ISAIAH 55:3, 10-11, NLT

The Word of God provides the reliable, soul-enriching nourishment we absolutely cannot do without. As Peter said,

> We also have the prophetic message as something completely reliable, and you will do well to pay attention to it, as to a light shining in a dark place, until the day dawns and the morning star rises in your hearts. Above all, you must understand that no prophecy of Scripture came about by the prophet's own interpretation of things. For prophecy never had its origin in the human will, but prophets, though human, spoke from God as they were carried along by the Holy Spirit.
>
> 2 PETER 1:19-21

As we try to listen for the voice of God and the leading of the Holy Spirit, we can tune our ears to hear God's voice accurately by reading the Bible. Paul said, "All Scripture is God-breathed and is useful for teaching, rebuking, correcting and training in righteousness, so that the servant of God may be thoroughly equipped for every good work" (2 Timothy 3:16-17). Nothing the Holy Spirit reveals today will ever contradict something the Holy Spirit already has revealed.

For this reason, we must carefully test what we think God

is showing us today. "Dear friends, do not believe every spirit, but test the spirits to see whether they are from God, because many false prophets have gone out into the world" (1 John 4:1). The simplest test of discernment is to compare what you are "hearing" from the Lord to the written Word of God. "Do not stifle the Holy Spirit. Do not scoff at prophecies, but test everything that is said. Hold on to what is good" (1 Thessalonians 5:19-21, NLT). If what you hear matches the Bible, then your confidence may increase. If the Bible contradicts what you "hear," you may be sure that you heard wrong.

Back when I first started to pursue an ability to get clear guidance from God's Spirit, I served in a student ministry with distinct charismatic leanings. In worship one day, someone gave a prophecy: "We need to stop putting God in a box," a man said. After I pondered his prophetic words for a while, I realized that the Bible was his "box." He meant that God would reveal things to us today that would contradict the Bible.

It so shocked me to see everyone lapping up this idea that I interrupted him with a shout: "But the Bible is the only clear revelation we have from God! It's the only thing we can be sure about!" Everyone in the crowd had been hanging on his every word, so my outburst stunned them. Every eye shot my way, bulging in surprise. I felt embarrassed for publicly losing it. A long, pregnant pause stretched out as everyone awkwardly glanced around.

The worship leader saved the moment, suddenly breaking out in furious strumming. He played a rousing acoustic worship chorus to recover the lost mood provoked by my Jesus-flipping-tables-in-the-Temple moment. Everyone thought I was crazy, but looking back, I give my young, naive self a standing ovation for that outburst. I'm glad that a fundamental

Protestant Christian worldview theme shot straight out of my mouth.

I have found this notion to be rock-solid reliable for my life and leadership. We can't migrate away from the Bible without devastating the body of Christ. I have learned that when a person starts expounding some theology that he or she says has matured beyond the limits of the Bible, sin lurks close by.

When we human beings strive to hear from God without the guardrails of the Bible, Satan soon persuades us to sin. As Paul explains: "Their destiny is destruction, their god is their stomach, and their glory is in their shame. Their mind is set on earthly things" (Philippians 3:19). In extraordinary hearing, one of the objects of the game is to never contradict Scripture. Steeping our lives in Scripture daily safeguards us.

How Much Is the Bible Worth to You?

What is the Bible worth to you? If you had never seen a Bible in English, how much would you pay for one? Would you trade your car or your house? I'm sure you highly value the Word, but do you value it enough to give a half hour every day to read it? That's the pattern that reveals the true value you place on the Bible.

God says, "Fix these words of mine in your hearts and minds . . . Teach them to your children, talking about them when you sit at home and when you walk along the road, when you lie down and when you get up" (Deuteronomy 11:18-19). God wants us to put His Word at the very core of our lives.

Without regularly engaging Scripture in your life, it's not safe to practice extraordinary hearing. As Jesus said, "Your mistake is that you don't know the Scriptures, and you don't know the power of God" (Mark 12:24, NLT). In this book, we strive to know both the Scriptures *and* the way God moves in power around us. When we regularly engage Scripture, we can expect the Word of God to plow and prepare the soil of our hearts.

Here's Your Job

Not more than two or three weeks into my life among the Yalunka people, Sayon, the leader of the Yalunka church, sat me down to explain life to me. "Now, your job is to watch what we do in the church," Sayon said, "and let us know if there is anything we are doing that isn't in the Bible." I thought, *I like my job.*

Sitting next to him, the pastor told me, "Also, you are going to preach every sermon until you learn the language." Now, *that's* motivation. For two years I worked full-time on learning the language and preaching in French, which an interpreter then translated into Yalunka.

After two years, I finally began to preach in Yalunka. I returned to the leaders for a revision of my job description.

"Listen," I said, "I studied in missionary school that the local people are supposed to preach in church, not foreign missionaries."

They looked back at me skeptically and queried, "What good is it to have a missionary if he doesn't *do* anything?" That zinged home.

With a fair bit of negotiation, we agreed that I would preach on Sunday morning, and they would take the other three preaching slots during the week: Thursday night, Saturday night, and Sunday night.

When Rebecca and I finally learned Yalunka, we began to work as a team with the church to translate the Bible. Desperate for content, every Sunday I would preach what we translated. Surrounded by people who follow the Quran, we chose to start with Genesis, because everyone had heard stories from the Quran about Adam, Noah, Abraham, Isaac, and Joseph.

One Saturday as I prepared my sermon, I felt dismayed to find that we had come to the story about Noah getting drunk and laying naked in his tent. I had resolved to skip it until I saw that the whole next chapter contained genealogies. I determined to skip that too. I mean, who preaches genealogies?

Down in the pit of my stomach I felt something that could have been my conscience. I thought, *Greg, you are a Bible translator. You don't believe that there are any vestigial parts of the Bible—Scriptures inspired by God for no purpose—do you? All Scripture is God-breathed. You need to figure out why these stories are in the Bible and preach that.*

I walked out the door and started talking to my neighbors about the story of naked Noah. They recognized it immediately, "Yes, of course, that's when Noah cursed his son and he turned black. That's where African people come from." I don't know if I managed to keep the look of horror from my face. I knew right away that *this* was the satanic lie that God had designed these chapters to correct.

The next morning, I felt very unsure what would happen during the sermon. I got up and read the story of Noah and his sons in Genesis 9. But the story took an unexpected turn for the church when I read the words in Yalunka, "*N bata Kanan danga,*" which in English reads, "Cursed be Canaan!" (Genesis 9:25). Instead of cursing Ham, the son who disgraced him, the text says Noah cursed Canaan, one of Ham's sons (Noah's grandson). Canaan's descendants later were conquered by Israel and had nothing to do with Africa. That's where the curse ends.

We looked ahead to the genealogy in Genesis 10:6 to find that Cush, the ancestor of the African peoples, had no involvement in the curse at all. Cush was Canaan's oldest brother. The never-cursed Cush went on to have descendants who became African emperors, some of them occasionally ruling Egypt from the upper reaches of the Nile River (2 Kings 19:9). *These* were the ancestors of the Yalunka people.

No sooner had I explained all that than a man in the back of the church leapt to his feet and said, "Wait a minute! If what you are saying is true, that means that Canaan was cursed, not Cush. Wouldn't that mean that *we* aren't under the curse of Noah?" Eyes wide at the interruption, I stammered, "Yes."

As I sucked in a breath to deliver the next point of my sermon, another man bolted to his feet and shouted, "Hey! That means that all of us here, we *aren't cursed*! Right?"

I had started to question the clarity of my message when a third guy jumped to his feet and said, "So you mean to say that *we* aren't cursed by God?" My face must have seemed a mask of puzzlement by this point, as I nodded wordlessly.

Then, right down on the front row, a quieter voice, trembling with age, interrupted. The long-retired, venerated pastor, Daniel, didn't stand up to object because that would have taken far too long. "Wait a minute," he mused aloud. "If I understand you, you mean to say that God didn't curse *us*." I turned to him in his special seat of honor at the front of the church and repeated the fourth confirmation. "Yes, that's what the Bible says."

Daniel got a faraway look in his eye as his mind wandered to all the times the elevated infant mortality in his village had stolen a baby from a young family. He thought about the many hundreds of relatives he had buried who had suffered under the crushing load of chronic malaria and cholera. A thousand sorry examples of brutal poverty played out in his mind behind his pensive eyes. He and his fathers had seen years of famine so bad that people would cook termite mounds and wild yams to stave off death. With a haunted look, he turned back to pose the question, "Then how *do* you explain it?"

Until that moment, it had all made so much sense to them. Every time a child died of malnutrition or malaria, every hunger pang, it all boiled down to the burden of God's curse on Africa. With just one story and one genealogy from Genesis, Pastor Daniel began to reconsider his entire worldview. If they weren't cursed by God—if that could be true—then, maybe, it all didn't *have* to be that way. Maybe, just maybe, Africa *could* rise. Maybe we really could drill wells, plant orchards, and change everything. Maybe little African children needn't always suffer hunger. Maybe Africans could work their way out of poverty under a shower of divine blessings instead of a curse.

At that moment, I saw people in the church begin to change from fatalistic to futuristic. They became men and women of great vision. They are now the kind of people who will look out at dozens of acres on top of a hill and gesture around expansively as they say, "I think we can plant all this with cashews and fence it."

The Word of God has power, even in its strange stories about naked, cursing men. Even in genealogies. When the Yalunka studied the Bible for themselves, they came to know who *they* really are and who *God* really is.

Before you marvel at the story and miss the point, think about yourself. The culture surrounding us promotes lies just as destructive. What does God intend for you, your family, and your country? What is sexuality all about? Why should I work? You won't ever really know unless you read the Bible.

"People do not live by bread alone, but by every word that comes from the mouth of God" (Matthew 4:4, NLT). Without the Word, you can't live—at least, not really. You won't live the vibrant spiritual life God intended unless you rise above the lies of the world that hold us down.

Open up the Word and read it for yourself. The *R* in PROACTIVE stands for read.

Discussion Questions

1. What do you think your life would be like without Scripture translated into your own language?
2. What have you learned from the Bible that has changed your life?
3. How do you think a daily habit of reading the Bible might further transform you?
4. How would a daily habit of Bible reading help you hear from God or evaluate what you hear?
5. What's the difference between reading the Bible for knowledge and reading the Bible to know the Author?
6. How do you personally make sure to "open the door" to fellowship with Jesus while you read the Bible?
7. How will you build a Scripture-reading habit in your life, starting this week?

CHAPTER 6

OBEY

Blessed rather are those who hear the word of God and obey it.

LUKE 11:28

P R O A C T I V E
b
e
y

WE HADN'T INTENDED to cast out demons and get people baptized, but that's just what happens when people read the Bible for themselves, discover what it means, and obey it. The mission method we call Discovery Bible Study unleashes that kind of power.

The year was 2018. We already had finished translating the whole Bible four years earlier, but the project hadn't ended for us. Pioneer Bible Translators won't stop until we see a network of churches using the translated Scriptures to grow, mature, and multiply—not an easy task among people who follow the Quran. So, often, Rebecca and I go to West Africa to help train local people to become disciples who make disciples. We hope that a great movement of Christ followers will multiply across the Yalunka region as Discovery Bible Studies get started and groups of people gather weekly to study and obey the Bible translated into Yalunka.

We gathered about twenty-five people from seven villages to experience Discovery Bible Studies. We had both third generation Christians and enthusiastic new seekers. Since only about half of them could read, we used a solar-powered device from Faith Comes By Hearing[12] to play the dramatized audio of the book of Matthew, one chapter at a time. I wrote seven questions on the board. As we listened to each chapter, a different person got up each time to take their turn leading the group through a discussion of our seven questions:

1. What did you like about this story?
2. What did you not like, or what was hard to understand about the story?
3. What do we learn about people from this?
4. What do we learn about God from this?
5. How will we change our lives to obey this teaching?
6. What is the name of the person you will share this with?
7. After our last study, how did it go when you shared the story with someone?

I had preached for years on baptism. I wrote some true classics of the Christian faith about baptism in Yalunka and preached them, but to my irritation, some of the key people attending our church had never chosen to get baptized. As if their belief system had been sealed with a nonstick Teflon coating, my baptism sermons just slid right off.

I remember getting so revved up trying to persuade people to get baptized that I preached part of one sermon from outside the door of the church. Every neck craned around, trying to follow my animated movements. Suddenly, I raced around the side of the church to preach through the window, as escalating shock registered on every face. "Baptism is a little like the doorway for entering the faith," I said. "Why would you try to come in the window when Jesus already has clearly shown us the door?"

No one felt impressed enough to actually get baptized.

When we got to Matthew chapter 3 and asked question number five of the seven Discovery Bible Study questions—"How will you change your life to obey this teaching?"—it floored me to hear one of the men say, "I have never been baptized, and John the Baptist said to be baptized. So today, right when this class is over, we're all going down to the river and I'm getting baptized." This very person had sleepily nodded through all my heart-racing preaching on baptism. I thought, *Really? Now? After all these years, all it takes is to listen to a chapter of the Bible and ask how you will obey it, and now you want to get baptized?*

Three people got baptized on that first day of the workshop.

I secretly felt miffed.

But the Bible is powerful! It's hard to compete with it.

On day two of the workshop, we reached the part where we asked the seventh question: "Yesterday when you shared the story with someone else, how did it go?" Another man said, "I walked home to my village last night, and I told my wife and family everything. I told them about the three people who got baptized. And my family said, 'Why didn't you get baptized too?' And I said, 'I don't know.' So today, at the end of this class, we are all going down to the river and I'm getting baptized."

Really, I thought, *that's what it takes to spur you to action? Question number seven of the Discovery Bible Study method did the job for you?*

Before this man decided to follow Jesus, he had been oppressed by a demon. I tell the story of how God delivered him in chapter 10. When the church interceded for him, God instantly delivered him of evil spirits. He attended church. He, too, endured hours of my oratory efforts without ever getting baptized. Yet here he finally decided to get baptized, just from the simple process of listening to the Bible, discovering what it means in group discussion, and talking about how to obey it together with the group and with his family.

It just so happened that, about a month before the workshop, one of the new people learning to follow Jesus also had become oppressed by a demon. Notice I don't talk about "demon possession," as our English translations call it. In the Greek New Testament, the presence and influence of a demon are not described as a person being "possessed." The Bible usually says the person is "demonized" or that the person "has a demon."

Christians can be influenced by demons, especially if they consciously play around with sin, but the presence of the Holy Spirit in their lives prevents them from becoming "demon possessed." This man was one of the new, energetic evangelists, but still was battling an addiction to drugs. One day he fell into temptation, abused some substance, and suddenly went out of his mind. The oldest Yalunka church sent a group to pick him up in a car, brought him back to their home village, and spent about a month praying for him and delivering him from the influence of drugs and demons.

He, too, got healed just in time for the workshop. The demons left him alone. He returned to his sound state of mind.

His extended family felt so impressed with his deliverance

from the demons that they sent another young man under demonic oppression to the Discovery Bible Study workshop, hoping to have the demons driven away from him too. And yes, it became distracting. He kept hopping up and briskly walking out, only to get ushered back in by his relatives.

That's how, to my surprise, the seminar became a deliverance ministry event. At the end of each day, we tacked on a prayer session and commanded the demons to leave him, in Jesus' name. In West Africa, that's how we roll.

When we came to Matthew 12:43-45, all three of these men who had suffered from demons listened intently. That's the section in which Jesus explains that when an impure spirit is cast out, it returns later with seven other spirits more wicked than itself . . . if the person's life remains empty. When we listened to Matthew 12 and asked what we learn about people from the story (question number three), the first formerly demon-oppressed man started giving his whole testimony. He explained how he had been so attacked by demons that he couldn't eat or drink for twelve days. He told about the church driving away the demons and how even his epilepsy eventually was brought under greater control.

The younger man suffering the influence of demons hung on his every word. At the end of the class, we prayed for him and drove away the demons. Then, both formerly demon-oppressed men went right down to the river to get baptized together to fill their lives with Jesus and keep the spirits from returning. I watched in awe as all three formerly demon-oppressed men discussed how to obey the Bible together.

I'm not embarrassed to admit that on day three of the workshop, when nobody got delivered of evil spirits or baptized, I felt a bit disappointed. I had come to expect huge spiritual power to get released simply by listening to Scripture and asking these simple questions. Maybe more transformations were happening that I couldn't see?

By the end of the workshop, we said to the thirty people, "Now, go out to your home villages and do there what we did here."

We got a call a week later. They already had started sharing the Bible with a group in a village where the gospel message had never been proclaimed. The Word of God has power to transform lives!

So what about you? Have *you* encountered the power that comes from discovering what the Word of God means?

Personal Discovery Bible Study

If we are going to learn to hear from God, we must build a pattern of discovering the meaning of the Bible and learning to obey it. If we find just one thing to change about our lives daily, over the years we will grow more Christlike.

If we serve God without the continual correction of the Word, however, we will gradually veer off course—maybe even by just one degree. Traveling in a slightly wrong direction over time will eventually get us tragically lost. As Moses explained, "Take to heart all the words I have solemnly declared to you this day, so that you may command your children to obey carefully all the words of this law. They are not just idle words for you—they are your life" (Deuteronomy 32:46-47).

When you read or listen to the Bible, try being guided by the questions we use in the Discovery Bible Study:[13] What do I learn about God? What will I do differently today because I read this Scripture this morning? Was I faithful yesterday to share what I learned from the Scriptures? With whom will I share this passage and its teaching as I go about my business today?

Obeying God's Word lays a crucial foundation for being able to hear from God and receive guidance from the Spirit. Jesus said,

> Anyone who loves me will obey my teaching. My Father will love them, and we will come to them and make our home with them. Anyone who does not love me will not obey my teaching. . . . But the Advocate, the Holy Spirit, whom the Father will send in my name, will teach you all things and will remind you of everything I have said to you.
>
> JOHN 14:23-26

If God has given us commands in His Word and we do not obey them, Jesus says we don't love Him. But as we *do* love and obey Jesus, He promises the Holy Spirit will teach us all things.

It makes sense. If God already has given you one message and you didn't obey it, why would He give you another one? He's still waiting on the obedience you owe Him from the first message!

We have a whole Bible full of God's teaching to read and obey. That's why reading and obeying the Scriptures prepares our hearts for extraordinary hearing. We learn to obey what God already has revealed in the Bible; then He gives us further instructions.

Spiritual Object Permanence

Have you ever noticed that we human beings are not very gifted at obeying God? Recently when reading Exodus, I noticed that God's people are capable of stunning disobedience.

It might seem logical to assume that if people witness a great miracle of God, they will become more obedient; but the Bible doesn't paint the picture that way.

The Israelites in the book of Exodus witnessed the full glory of the ten plagues, some of the greatest miracles in history. In Exodus 15:21, the people of God sang about how God had hurled the Egyptian army to the bottom of the sea. But just three verses later, they "turned against Moses" because they had nothing to drink. A month went by, and they continued to moan and groan: "If only the LORD had killed us back in Egypt" (Exodus 16:3, NLT). "Ah, Egypt," they sighed, "where we sat around huge pots of meat and sauntered through all-you-can-eat buffets." They cast an accusing finger at the miraculous pillar of cloud that had led them out of Egypt, squinted into the glare and shimmering heat waves of the wilderness, and wailed, "*You* have brought us into the desert to starve us all to death."

Imagine God's indignation! Here He had just worked the greatest signs and wonders in all of history. The ten plagues brought Pharaoh to his knees. The parting of the Red Sea ushered His people safely out of Egypt and redeemed them from slavery. The army of one of the great superpowers of the ancient world sank to the bottom of the sea, special-forces chariots and all. And barely a month later, the Israelites' attitude had become, "What have you done for us lately?"

How did God hold back His anger?

We have a lot in common with them. We tend to lack what I call "spiritual object permanence."

Have you ever played with an infant and showed them a toy? Their little eyes lock onto that toy like lasers. Then you move it behind a blanket, and it's just gone. The baby has no idea the toy is still there. It ceases to exist as soon as it moves out of sight.

When they get to be about six months old, they start to get clever; they realize that just because they can't see it doesn't mean it winked out of existence.

To God, we are like babies who forget yesterday's miracles and commands as soon as they move out of sight. We shake our fist at heaven, saying, "Yes, God, but what have you done for me today?" Those blessings have passed behind the hazy veil of a short attention span. For all practical purposes, they no longer exist.

Spiritually, we need to develop beyond the maturity of a six-month-old baby. We need spiritual object permanence. Yes, God gave the Ten Commandments to Moses some 3,500 years ago, but spiritually, those 3,500 years don't change anything. God remains the same, while we change every day. Until we begin to mature in our long-term obedience, our relationship with the eternal God will remain strained.

Have you noticed that our churches seem to constantly pursue the next big thing? The biggest churches invent something, then all the megachurches cycle that innovation through their pulpits as the next big thing. Then the smaller churches try their best to emulate it. But have you noticed that the next big thing is never simply "Obey Jesus"? That's not glamorous enough to catch our attention, even though so much hinges on it.

Our churches and our pastors need us to become more constant, more unwavering. If God commanded it once, we don't need Him to command it again in a more entertaining way. Right now, take a moment to decide for yourself to commit to the blessed simplicity of reading and obeying the Bible every day.

Eternally Durable, Infinitely Valuable

Years ago, in West Africa, I had the privilege of presenting to my Christian neighbor, Mr. Camara, the first translation we did of the New Testament in his language. Not long afterward, he brought a young couple to my front porch to get the wife's swollen eye treated. I felt upset because I could see that the man had beaten his wife—tragically, not unusual in that part of the world.

Mr. Camara gently explained to the man my angry reaction: "The time for beating your wife is past."

Stunned, the man countered, "Wait a minute! If you can't beat your wife anymore, how can you keep her from doing bad things?"

Mr. Camara's weathered face glowed with joy as he elaborated, "The thing that tells us not to beat our wives is the same thing that tells them not to do bad things."

That "thing" is the Bible in their language. When Mr. Camara said, "The time for beating your wife is past," that was just his way of saying, "The Kingdom of God has come among us. The Bible in our language has ushered in a new era in our history: a time when husbands love their wives, when parents care for their children; a time when Jesus is King." I watched God's Word in their language transform their hearts!

Jesus said, "Heaven and earth will pass away, but my words will never pass away" (Mark 13:31). The Word of God is more durable and valuable than all the splendor of heaven and earth. The *O* in PROACTIVE stands for obey.

Discussion Questions

1. Describe some moments in your life when you seemed to lack "spiritual object permanence." How did it impact you?
2. What commands of Jesus are the hardest for you to obey? Why?
3. How does disobedience make extraordinary hearing harder?
4. How does reading and obeying the Bible open the door to extraordinary hearing?
5. How do you plan to apply the Discovery Bible Study questions in your own personal Bible reading?

CHAPTER 7

ADORE

Holy, holy, holy is the LORD Almighty; the whole earth is full of his glory.

ISAIAH 6:3

P R O A C T I V E
d
o
r
e

WALKING ON TRAILS after dark in Africa scares me. Oh, I try to act tough. As a Texan, I would rather die than look weak. So I pretend like nothing's happening, boldly strolling down the shadowy, partially brush-covered pathway that leads from my house to the church, as my flashlight beam nervously twitches from shadow to shadow, dispelling terrors. I go first in line, and then I tuck Rebecca right in behind me, both of us whipping our lights like pistols toward any twig-snapping sound.

Our anxieties are well-founded. On these very pathways lurk rats the size of a small dog. We have killed more than one five-foot-long spitting cobra. So far as I know, that garden-hose-long green mamba still slinks around out there somewhere. He's a wily one. I never can quite get the shotgun loaded and trained on him in time to send him to the snake afterlife.

Let's not even talk about the spiders.

Every Thursday, Saturday, and Sunday night, the Yalunka believers in West Africa hold a church service. Lately they have added a 5:30 a.m. service every day, so that's a lot of cowering trips to church, feigning bravery in the dark.

The church building sits at the bottom of a hill, a small, baked-brick structure with weathered, wooden benches sanded glassy smooth by years of people's behinds scooting along their length to make room for the next worshiper. The rafters are rough-hewn and uneven. The building boasts no ceiling to intercede between the worshipers and the metal roof above. A light source must always brighten the front of the church during every nighttime service; it's an inalienable responsibility of the leader who directs worship.

Throughout each service, those of us who can read shine our flashlights intently on our hymnals or Bibles. Curious clouds of insects flitter persistently around each circle of glare. I have old copies of the Yalunka Scriptures that sport decades-old, dried termites permanently pressed into the pages, highlighting with their wings the supporting texts of myriad past sermon points.

One night I remember being a little absentminded as I strolled down to church, walked in, and began the ritual for sitting down on the bench. With the speed of subconscious thought, I vigilantly shined the flashlight behind and under the bench. I glanced at the rafters above and the concrete floor below. Only after feeling reassured that I hadn't cozied up to a skulking roach or a stately, spreading wall spider did I plop down on the bench. My African colleagues entered and stoically sat down without the least concern. My Texan soul begrudgingly admired their superiority.

But on this night, we would all be equal. None of us had the least inkling of a problem developing for the first part of the service. We didn't know that unseen invaders had penetrated our security.

You may need to stop reading for a moment and google "driver ants." When I tapped out those words in Google's query bar, a convenient series of suggested common questions popped up: "Can driver ants eat humans? Are driver ants dangerous? What is the most dangerous ant in the world?" I didn't need to click on any of that. I grasp the answers to these questions on a visceral level.

Driver ants are among the most democratic of the African insects, rigorously treating each human being with magnanimous equality. They roam about West Africa in swarms of approximately one gazillion ants patrolling for protein—including you, even if you are an American citizen. When you step into their swarm unaware, they fluidly glide up your body with ease. But they don't bite—no, not at first. The entire horde harbors but one patient ambition: to make their way to the waistband of your undergarments.

When a quorum of ants forms around your waistline, one intrepid insect puts out a signal. I'm not entirely clear how the science works, but upon the blowing of this little ant-trumpet, every individual strikes with boundless savagery, pouring out all the malice their wicked little souls can muster upon your skin. As it happens, many of the ants do not appear to arrive at their intended destination, stinging the body at pretty much any unexpected location. The largest members of the swarm come standardly equipped with imposing pincers, with which they cling tenaciously to whatever part of your skin they can reach.

On this most unfortunate moonless night, a massive horde of driver ants apparently had chosen to migrate right in front of the church entrance. The ants went entirely undetected through the opening prayer and well into the first song. That's when the formic acid flew.

Suddenly, my eyes flew wide open as my hand shot involuntarily down to my waist. The song, now punctuated throughout the building by unrhythmic slaps on shoulder blades and swats on pant legs as each worshiper made the jolting discovery at the same moment, continued.

It never rose to the level of an emergency that would stop the service. When it comes to insects, after all, these believers are the most battle-hardened of God's saints. They tried to appear as if they all nonchalantly continued to focus on worship—but their eyes betrayed other more pressing concerns. Throughout the songs and well into the sermon, a sudden, random slap would break the silent concentration of the body of Christ as late-arriving driver ants announced their intentions long after the main body of invaders already had been pinched and rolled between fingers in the cloth of everyone's clothes.

After church, we couldn't stop laughing about it. For a while, it looked as though the whole church had gotten the Holy Ghost in fits and starts.

Do You Struggle with Worship?

Do you struggle worshiping God? Worship is hard for me. As Christians, we set out with good intentions, but daily life can interfere. We want to experience that holy, awestruck moment in God's presence, but the distractions of our lives intrude like uninvited driver ants in church.

Yet human beings seem to enter the world with an inclination to worship. Go outside at night, stare up at the starry expanse, and see what happens in your heart as you look up and think about the One who made all those stars. That sense of wonderment that sweeps over you doesn't come from the backward tilt of your head as you look up. It's the beginning of worship. Something like that involuntary experience of awe may explain why virtually all human cultures have a persistent belief in a god.

People tend to believe they *should* worship. I've seen a rural family sacrificing a ram to a huge tree in a forest in West Africa. In a rice field in India, the local people told me about worshiping at a lonely, spreading tree beside the road. On a deeply forested hillside in Asia, I watched a group of men play instruments and sacrifice a chicken before a tree in order to persuade a god to come down to bless their village with rain. They told me that their ancestors had bowed before that same tree for more than four hundred years.

Left to their own devices, people find awe-inspiring explanations for the beauty of creation around them, and then they worship . . . something. They know something unseen deserves to share that moment of awe as they ponder creation.

But in the same way that city lights blur the magnificence of the stars at night and human populations clear away dense jungles, so our sense of wonder steadily erodes as we surround ourselves with things made by people. In our modern, hurried, indoor, air-conditioned world, we insulate ourselves from the fascinating wonder of God and His creation, replacing worship with other loyalties.

On the internet, we get to remake ourselves into whatever we want. We spin facts and events into our own fantasy of what the world should be. We gradually forget a crucial truth: *we* are not God. We do not control creation. We do not make ourselves and the world in our own image.

Worship calls us back to a clear picture of who we are and who He is.

How could we hear from a God whom we do not worship? We need adoration in our lives to put us in the proper position to hear from Him.

Worship means bowing heart and body before God in proper response to who He is and what He has done. In the Old Testament, worship is frequently displayed either in serving God or in bowing to the ground before Him. Worship includes a total submission of our lives.

In the New Testament, the main word translated "worship" means to bow down in reverence. The basic idea of worship includes expressing how awestruck we feel by how much greater, higher, and more powerful God is than us.

Don't Forget to Worship

Jesus taught that prayer includes worship. The prayer that Jesus modeled for His disciples in Matthew 6:9-13 includes worship right at the start with the words, "hallowed be your name." Worship can often include the physical act of bowing before God, but it *must* include the spiritual act of submitting the heart to God.

Jesus explained, "Yet a time is coming and has now come when the true worshipers will worship the Father in the Spirit and in truth, for they are the kind of worshipers the Father seeks" (John 4:23). We live in that time; we who follow Jesus have the opportunity to grow into the kind of worshipers that God has always wanted.

Worship is not supposed to feel exhausting. At times in our religious zeal, we can multiply the number of activities and hours scheduled and place expectations on people to show enormous exuberance. It seems spiritual to talk about praying all night and getting up early to allow for more hours of spiritual time. But watch out! God closely links worship to rest in the Bible. The very day of worship in the Bible was called the Sabbath, a day to rest and renew before the following workweek (Exodus 20:8-11). The soul at rest worships.

Acts of genuine worship give life and rest. Approaching God to hear from Him does not require unsustainable levels of prayer and worship. As Jesus said, "Come to me, all of you who are weary and carry heavy burdens, and I will give you rest" (Matthew 11:28, NLT). The pattern of worship that leads to extraordinary hearing includes restful, life-giving time in God's presence, praising Him.

How to Worship Well

While all human beings seem preprogrammed to want to worship, we don't seem especially gifted to worship *well.* When we get alone with God, we often don't seem to know exactly what to *do* to worship God in the Spirit and in truth.

Scripture itself provides the best guide. As I work my way through the memory device PROACTIVE during my daily devotional times, when I get to the *A* (adore), that's my moment to take some time to worship God. I would not actually know what to do without the worship recorded in the book of Revelation. The celestial beings described there have far more experience in worship than we do. So I use some of their words. Why don't you join me in practicing this form of worship?

Find a quiet place. If you can, get down on your knees or lie flat on the ground. Let your mind roam and imagine freely how elevated and powerful the God who created the earth must be. Speak out loud these words:

> Holy, holy, holy is the Lord God, the Almighty—the one who always was, who is, and who is still to come.
>
> REVELATION 4:8, NLT

> You are worthy, O Lord our God, to receive glory and honor and power. For you created all things, and they exist because you created what you pleased.
>
> REVELATION 4:11, NLT

> You are worthy to take the scroll and break its seals and open it. For you were slaughtered, and your blood has ransomed people for God from every tribe and language and people and nation. And you have caused them to become a Kingdom of priests for our God. And they will reign on the earth.
>
> REVELATION 5:9-10, NLT

> Worthy is the Lamb who was slaughtered—to receive power and riches and wisdom and strength and honor and glory and blessing.
>
> REVELATION 5:12, NLT

> Blessing and honor and glory and power belong to the one sitting on the throne and to the Lamb forever and ever.
>
> REVELATION 5:13, NLT

Amen! Blessing and glory and wisdom and thanksgiving and honor and power and strength belong to our God forever and ever! Amen.

REVELATION 7:12, NLT

Great and marvelous are your works, O Lord God, the Almighty. Just and true are your ways, O King of the nations. Who will not fear you, Lord, and glorify your name? For you alone are holy. All nations will come and worship before you, for your righteous deeds have been revealed.

REVELATION 15:3-4, NLT

Praise the LORD! For the Lord our God, the Almighty, reigns. Let us be glad and rejoice, and let us give honor to him. For the time has come for the wedding feast of the Lamb, and his bride has prepared herself. She has been given the finest of pure white linen to wear.

REVELATION 19:6-8, NLT

When I say those words aloud to God, I cannot remain unmoved. God becomes so great in my mind that He fills my thoughts. Earthly distractions get shoved roughly aside by my expanding awareness of the presence of the Creator of the universe.

Suddenly, I am ready to encounter the irrefutable guidance of the Holy Spirit, unchallenged by rational objections born of faithless human reason. It makes my soul ready for extraordinary hearing because my awareness opens to the presence of an extraordinary God.

Worship has become one of the only times of day I can be

sure that I'm not sinning. At times, I feel so beaten down by life and work that it seems no matter what I say, it feels wrong. At those times, I remember Proverbs 10:19: "Too much talk leads to sin" (NLT). And I talk for a living!

But when I worship, I suddenly feel relief to sense that, even if every other word I have spoken recently went wrong and may even have been a sin, at least this one thing I can be sure is right. When my soul calls out praises to God, no sin lives in those words. Far from it, they are the *most* right things to say. They must be if angels invest all eternity shouting worshipful words.

So at least once in my day, I try to join my voice with theirs: "God, you are great. God, I worship you. Lord, I love you. Lord, you made the stars. Lord, you made the earth." It's the simplest, most childlike, and most truthful moment of my day.

Discussion Questions

1. Have you ever tried to establish a daily pattern of worship? If so, how did it go?
2. When you worship, what activities do you find truly powerful?
3. Which everyday worries of life tend to intrude on your worship?
4. How much time should we take to worship so that the worship suits God's glory but also fits into the schedule of a sustainable, restful life?
5. How do you think worshiping God every day might impact how you hear from God?

6. Take time right now to list some things for which you worship God. Use this sentence: "I worship you, God, because . . ."

CHAPTER 8

CONFESS

When I spoke, they did not listen. They deliberately sinned before my very eyes and chose to do what they know I despise.

ISAIAH 66:4, NLT

P R O A C T I V E
o
n
f
e
s
s

WHEN I WAS a tiny child, we owned a big dog named Ginger. She became the brother I never had. Together we ruled the tunnellike underworld beneath the willowy arches of the jasmine hedge that ran the full length of our back fence. As superheroes, we sprinted all over the yard, fighting entire world wars and alien invasions, armed only with imagination and sticks. We were inseparable, and I loved that dog dearly.

One day, when I was in about the second grade, Ginger and I were patrolling the neighborhood when she zeroed in on a particularly fascinating scent, as dogs tend to do. She headed straight over to a huge pile of dog mess with the kind of intense concentration normally displayed by concert violinists.

A dog will do some things that a person would never, *ever* do. And there, to my horror, Ginger began to persistently roll in the poop, focusing on getting it evenly spread over her right shoulder and grinding it into her fur as thoroughly as possible. When she finally rolled all the way over, energetically hopped up, and fell back into step with me, our relationship had changed.

Oh, I still loved Ginger; but from then on, I treated her differently. We could no longer play with the same carefree abandon. I no longer wanted to pet her with the same tender affection. Playful wrestling suddenly seemed out of the question.

Ginger had no idea why I had become so suddenly aloof. But by my human standards, she reeked. I could not associate with something that dirty, no matter how great my love for her. When we got home, my dad heroically saved the day with our garden hose.

Stop Rolling in Filth

We won't clearly hear from God until we stop rolling in filth. He wants to interact with us. He loves us. But He just can't intermingle with the constant mess and corruption we introduce into our lives. It separates us from Him. We need a proper hosing off.

We must learn to stop returning to the stink of the habitual sin in our lives. Living a holy life puts us in a position to walk with God and practice extraordinary hearing.

Just like that story about my dog, a person will do some things that God would never, *ever* do. He's totally set apart from us and our earthly nature. That's the meaning of the word "holy."[14] He's simply not like us.

God could never feel tempted to steal money because He made and owns the whole of creation. He cannot see a reason to lie. What would He gain? He does not overeat. He could never become addicted to alcohol because He remains unaltered by any effect of time, matter, or substance. He cannot feel tempted to lust after one of the people He made, no matter how beautiful.

His fundamental nature is so completely and utterly distinct from and outside of His creation that He has no use for sin. How could He make creation if He did not already preexist it and live separate from it? He remains apart from the lowly elements of the creation, such as impurity, filth, and the mess of things related to bodily functions and death.

That's what we mean when we say that God is holy. He is set apart from sin, from purely earthly interests.

That's what so shocked us about Jesus, the Son of God, when He was born into this messy, lowly world. God left behind His separation from unholy things and brought His holiness into a dark and unspiritual place. He came to earth to make a way for us to live with Him in heaven. And in so doing, He made a way for *us* to be holy.

For human beings to be holy means that they, too, have been set apart for God's purposes from lowly, unclean, and sinful things. The problem between God and us comes when we who have been made holy by the blood of Jesus fall into sin.

The Scriptures compare sin to filth: "Of them the proverbs are true: 'A dog returns to its vomit,' and, 'A sow that is washed returns to her wallowing in the mud'" (2 Peter 2:22). What possible attraction could filth have to us, that we would keep coming back for more? I'm just like what Paul said: "I have discovered this principle of life—that when I want to do what is right, I inevitably do what is wrong . . . Oh, what a miserable person I am! Who will free me from this life that is dominated by sin and death?" (Romans 7:21, 24, NLT). The short answer is Jesus.

Unholiness Prevents Hearing

Even though Jesus saves us, we lowly human beings have a limited ability to hear from God and obey Him, due to the unholy parts of our lives. If we could eliminate sin from our lives, would we receive guidance from God as clearly as Jesus did? Maybe.

As we struggle to hear God's instructions, our sin acts like static on our spiritual radio, drowning out God's voice. Sin distracts us. As God told Jeremiah: "My people have not listened to me or even tried to hear. They have been stubborn and sinful" (Jeremiah 7:26, NLT). Sin and guilt can cause radio silence from God.

During the reign of King Saul, a time came when the king's erratic leadership style led to a moment of guilt right in the middle of a battle. When Saul tried to inquire of God, the text says, "God did not answer him that day" (1 Samuel 14:37). When King Saul began to sin habitually, God hung up the phone: "[Saul] inquired of the LORD, but the LORD did not answer him by dreams or Urim or prophets" (1 Samuel 28:6).

God told Ezekiel that He expected His people to choose Him over sin:

> Son of man, these men have set up idols in their hearts and put wicked stumbling blocks before their faces. *Should I let them inquire of me at all?*
>
> EZEKIEL 14:3

Ezekiel says that God won't let us inquire of Him when we insist on polluting ourselves:

> Do you intend to keep prostituting yourselves by worshiping vile images? . . . Should I allow you to ask for a message from me, O people of Israel? As surely as I live, says the Sovereign LORD, I will tell you nothing.
>
> EZEKIEL 20:30-31, NLT

I don't mean that God stops *loving* us when we find ourselves rolling in sin, over and over. Quite the contrary! Why did God tell Ezekiel that He refused to send messages to His people when they got mired in sin? He did this so He could "capture the minds and hearts of all" His people (Ezekiel 14:5, NLT). I think He remains silent so that we will choose what we want more in life—focusing on His voice or reveling in our sins. In His love, God always lets us choose.

The New Testament teaches that unholy living really means rejecting God:

> God's will is for you to be holy, so stay away from all sexual sin. . . . God has called us to live holy lives, not impure lives. Therefore, anyone who refuses to live by these rules is not disobeying human teaching *but is rejecting God*, who gives his Holy Spirit to you.
>
> 1 THESSALONIANS 4:3, 7-8, NLT

God does not reject us, but when we persist in unholiness, we repeatedly reject Him! God loves us too much to leave us uncorrected. Part of the correction includes waiting for us to leave our sins behind before He speaks more openly to us.

How, then, can we grow in our holiness to clear up the

static of sin that limits our hearing from God? We can all say at times, "What a miserable person I am!" (Romans 7:24, NLT). How do we leave behind old habits and hidden sins?

1. *Confess Sin to Clear the Static*

Confession begins the process of removing the distracting noise of sin that drowns out the divine whisper. The words usually translated "confess" in the New Testament are rooted in the idea "to say the same thing" as someone. Confessing sin is to say the same thing that God says about sin. John put it this way:

> If we claim we have no sin, we are only fooling ourselves and not living in the truth. *But if we confess our sins* to him, he is faithful and just to forgive us our sins and to cleanse us from all wickedness. If we claim we have not sinned, we are calling God a liar and showing that his word has no place in our hearts.
>
> 1 JOHN 1:8-10, NLT

Agreeing with God about sin is the first step to the holiness that opens the channel of communication between us and God. The Psalms explain it too:

> When I refused *to confess my sin*, my body wasted away, and I groaned all day long. . . . Finally, I confessed all my sins to you and stopped trying to hide my guilt. I said to myself, "I will confess my rebellion to the LORD." And you forgave me! All my guilt is gone.
>
> PSALM 32:3, 5, NLT

We can confess our faults not only to God, but also to one another. James says, "Therefore confess your sins to each other and pray for each other so that you may be healed" (James 5:16). Whether in public or through having an accountability partner, confession can help us overcome sin and grow in holiness.

2. *Put Sin to Death by the Spirit*

We see a tension in the Bible about how to be holy. In Leviticus, God says: "So *set yourselves apart* to be holy, for I am the LORD your God. Keep all my decrees by putting them into practice, for I am *the LORD who makes you* holy" (Leviticus 20:7-8, NLT). So do we make ourselves holy by keeping all His decrees? Or does God make us holy Himself? That passage says both.

Is it a question of willpower or divine intervention? In my experience, holiness requires both my best efforts and God's great power combined.

The apostle Paul teaches us to put sin to death by the Spirit: "For if you live according to the flesh, you will die; but *if by the Spirit you put to death the misdeeds of the body*, you will live" (Romans 8:13). So it's not just the Holy Spirit, and it's not just our willpower. He says that *you* must put your sins to death, but you do so by the power of the *Spirit* in your life. When we get trapped in a sin, we can commit aloud, "I am putting this sin to death by the power of the Spirit."

3. *Live Out the Truth*

Jesus prayed for you and me to become holy when He said, "Make them holy *by your truth*; teach them your word, which is truth. . . . I give myself as a holy sacrifice for them so they can be made holy *by your truth*" (John 17:17, 19, NLT). The truth about His sacrifice and about who we are in Him revolutionizes our habits.

What truth then *is* important for us to know so that we can become holy? We must understand the identity we already have received. We must know who we really are, and that Jesus *already* has finished making us holy when He died for us.

> For we know that our old self was crucified with him so that the body ruled by sin might be done away with, that we should no longer be slaves to sin—because anyone who has died has been set free from sin.
>
> ROMANS 6:6-7

We *already* have been set free from sin! The writer of Hebrews says, "We have *been made holy* through the sacrifice of the body of Jesus Christ once for all. . . . For by one sacrifice he has made perfect forever those who are *being made* holy" (Hebrews 10:10, 14). We "have been made holy" *and* we "are being made holy." Although we have a role in this process, we cannot render ourselves holy. Jesus already has made us holy! This is the truth that Jesus says will make us holy.

The remaining work is to consciously decide every moment not to contradict our true identity. We must live out the truth about ourselves. When we struggle with temptation, we must ask, "Is that who I am? Am I the father who betrays the mother of my children? Am I the guy who leads the charge of an organization and then falls into sin, bringing the whole thing crashing down? Am I the woman who talks about my friends behind their backs? Am I a verbally abusive mother? No! How could I contradict the truth about myself like that?"

We must decide to truly become the people Jesus already has made us to be, by His Spirit. Let's commit ourselves to making choices that resonate with our true identities. That truth surfaces in our lives as holiness.

4. Focus and Balance Physical Desires

Many of our sinful habits and addictions come from what the Bible calls "the flesh." Jesus sees the flesh and sees trouble: "It is the Spirit who gives life; the flesh is no help at all" (John 6:63, ESV). Paul describes our mighty struggle like this: "For the mind that is set on the flesh is hostile to God, for it does not submit to God's law; indeed, it cannot. Those who are in the flesh cannot please God" (Romans 8:7-8, ESV).

But what in the world is the "flesh," really? Sometimes the Bible uses *the flesh* as a theological idea to talk about "the sinful nature," our inherent, ingrained tendency to fall into sin. The term *flesh* also more broadly means anything having to do with the human body.

I have come to think about it mostly as the things our physical bodies want, our natural cravings. My body wants food, drink, beauty, sex, nice sensations, excitement, comfort, entertainment, caresses, escape, fantasy, power, rest, and even exercise. Unlike the sinful nature, God Himself put these natural "fleshly" desires in our bodies for good reason. But they must be:

1. managed in a careful balance, and
2. focused in the proper direction.

When we keep those two conditions, fleshly desires pose no problem. Through them we experience pleasure, comfort, and satisfaction. But focused in the wrong direction, or when they get out of balance, these cravings destroy us. That's when we leave behind the idea of "bodily cravings" and enter the territory of "the sinful nature."

You might feel tempted to say, "Oh Greg, you are so out of step with the times! We are more sophisticated now. We have discovered that these cravings aren't bad at all. Just go with it!" But if you do, you will find out, eventually, that the flesh out of balance will kill you: "For if you live according to the flesh you will die" (Romans 8:13, ESV). I don't need to make my point because the natural world ruthlessly reinforces the design of the Creator.

Thirst is good and drinking is good. But if I focus on drinking alcohol instead of water (focus in the wrong direction) and begin to drink too much (out of balance), I will damage my liver. Once out of balance and focus, I can become an alcoholic. My craving can eventually kill me.

Or what about food? Food is good. But if I focus on eating the wrong foods, I can begin to gain weight. When I eat out of balance with the rest of my life, eventually I become overweight. Then I can't sleep well because I snore at night. Lack of sleep leads to lack of energy and then to less exercise, then more overeating, obesity, and eventually a heart attack or stroke.

The flesh kills when out of balance and when wrongly focused.

How about sex? If I focus my sexual appetite on my wife and keep carefully balanced in a way that affirms and comforts her, my marriage grows sweeter every day. But if I were to become inflamed with desire for someone else, eventually I would destroy my marriage, and my wife and children would suffer.

Have you watched those "real crime" TV shows about a

wife who kills her cheating, lecherous husband? Rebecca and I watch those more than seems healthy. I could be wrong, but I suspect that my wife might approve of this very specific kind of murder.

The flesh out of balance, or focused in the wrong direction, kills.

That's how living for physical cravings can lead to addiction and death. Our culture champions the right to indulge these cravings, but the mortality and suicide rates associated with sinful addictions teach us that God is right. Holiness requires proper focus and balancing of physical cravings.

5. Be Content with God's Gifts

We overcome physical desires by enjoying the deep sense of peace and satisfaction we get from God's good, pleasing, and perfect gifts. Paul said it this way:

> I have learned how to be *content* with whatever I have. I know how to live on almost nothing or with everything. I have learned the secret of living in every situation, whether it is with a full stomach or empty, with plenty or little. For I can do everything through Christ, who gives me strength.
>
> PHILIPPIANS 4:11-13, NLT

Paul further clarifies, "But godliness *with contentment* is great gain. For we brought nothing into the world, and we can take nothing out of it. But if we have food and clothing, we will be *content with that*" (1 Timothy 6:6-8).

Sin exhausts the soul; its consequences drain us emotionally. Only holiness and holy activities truly give us rest and lead to a sustainable life. A key to holy living is learning contentment with the good things we already have. If I am at peace with my current station in life, then I won't overwork. I won't feel the craving for rest that assails me when I fill my life with frenetic activities. I won't feel overwhelmed by the need to medicate my stress by overindulging the natural cravings of my body. Godly contentment preempts sin.

If I learn to enjoy the wife God gave me, I won't ruin my marriage by lusting after other women. If I appreciate my children the way God made them, I won't ruin my relationship with them by nagging them to be like someone else. If I'm content with my home, my job, and the beautiful, loving connection I cultivate in my family and community, then I can look calmly at the sin and evil that crouches at my door to tempt me and say, "Nah, I don't need that."

I'm not saying we should be content with the evil state of this fallen creation! God Himself is not at peace with *that*. But you can love what God has given you and at the same time be filled with a passionate discontent with the evil that God opposes.

Experiment a little with godly contentment. Practice looking around your house and at your family through God's eyes. Watch your family intently and think, *Look at these gorgeous people God put in my life! They are fearfully and wonderfully made. I have enough.*

The only way we can fail to grow in holiness is to give up the fight. As we grow in holiness, the static will recede, and an extraordinary ability to hear God's voice will begin to grow.

Oh, to Be Less like Ginger!

It disturbs me how consistently my spiritual walk matches the behavior of my childhood dog, Ginger. I would like to tell you that I have advanced spiritually beyond the canine stage, but some days I wonder.

I remember a day when Ginger had grown much older. She and I were walking in our front yard together, as always. She normally stuck close to my side in adoration and fellowship. But I noticed at one point that she started getting a little too focused on circling around our street, chasing interesting smells. She didn't pay much attention to me or to my location. We no longer walked together. I began to call her to gently remind her that she was supposed to be *with me*.

Strangely, Ginger seemed to begin to pretend she couldn't hear me and gradually moved farther away. Ginger had episodes of rebellion and selective hearing.

As she sniffed her way farther down the street, I shouted louder and louder, to no avail. I remember watching her backside retreating farther and farther into the distance and thinking, *My dog is running away from home . . . again*. It happened sometimes. She wasn't 100 percent loyal to me.

I would always eventually get that lug of a dog wrestled back behind the fence. I would tirelessly sprint about, wave my arms, and yell. I would grab her by the collar and drag her rebellious hide back to our home. I would open the gate a crack and thrust her back into the yard, desperately blocking her exit with one leg while slamming the gate shut, barely pinching her nose as she fought to escape.

Why in the world would she leave? The bowl where we placed choice table scraps sat right there in the backyard. She had a whole family to dote on her. Why wasn't that enough? Why leave her home behind just to sniff around and get hit by a car? I couldn't ask her.

But I don't think I need to ask anymore. I see it all in myself.

Most days I'm loyal . . . but on a bad day, I struggle. It's not that God doesn't cry out after me. I just get too fascinated by the scent of the wide world to walk docilely by His side.

I once thought that if I worked at repentance long enough, as I grew older, I would find myself immune to the deadly attraction of the flesh and sin. But the longer I live, the more I realize that, on this earth, this fight will never fully end.

To truly walk with God and hear His voice, I need to maintain constant vigilance and to daily confess my sins. When we set up our PROACTIVE spiritual habits to plow the soil of our hearts daily, the *C* reminds us to invest time in confession.

Discussion Questions

1. How has wandering away from the Lord interfered with your ability to pray and hear from God?
2. How do you think confessing and eliminating sin from your life could help you better hear from God?
3. Name some of the most difficult cravings for you to keep focused in the right direction and in balance.
4. What have you found that helps you the most in overcoming those challenges?
5. With what parts of your life do you need to feel more content in order to overcome temptation?
6. To whom do you confess your sins to be healed, as James 5:16 directs?

CHAPTER 9

THANK

Give thanks to the LORD, for he is good! His faithful love endures forever.

PSALM 107:1, NLT

P R O A C T I V E
h
a
n
k

I MUST'VE BEEN four years old when I got my first enduring lesson about gratitude. My mother had taken me to a corrective shoe store. The man behind the counter had a treasure beyond reckoning for a child: little suckers in a jar. I wanted one *badly*.

But I had fallen into a sulky mood. I hated to buy shoes designed to straighten my stride. At the time, people believed that they could improve the way a child walked by shoes that gradually wrenched the child's feet into alignment. The doctor had instructed my mother to have my feet fitted with a pair of therapeutic bricks. You might think that people back then were just wrong about this, but watch me walk today. I have an immaculate gait.

The man could see me brooding. So to compensate for making my day worse, he reached out in a friendly gesture and offered me a plastic-wrapped sucker. Hot saliva instantly pooled in my mouth over that sugary, brittle candy. I intended to slurp loudly for hours on that cherry-sweet, red, sticky, plastic-textured, flat piece of heaven, right down to the papery-tasting stick. I craved chewing the paper stick until I soaked it free of flavor and it eventually began to dissolve into the kind of mess only a little boy knows how to properly create and deposit under the couch. Ravenous, I snatched it greedily.

My mother prompted me gently: "Greg, remember to say thank you." My fist clenched more tightly around the prize. My scowling eyes locked on the man suspiciously. I had no time for gratitude. My mother repeated her instruction, but my jaw clicked shut.

Mortified, my mother tensely encouraged me: "Greg, if you do not say thank you to this man, you cannot have that candy." My stubborn mind could not, would not respond with gratitude—not on this day. I set my face as flint against the world and darkly refused to express my thanks to that looming hulk behind the counter. Who was this man to steal *my* candy?

Sadly, I must report that, before I even realized she had moved, my mother had brusquely confiscated that sucker and handed it back to the man. Begrudgingly impressed at Mom's skills, I grumbled as I fell in line behind my siblings, stunned at the injustice of this world. My mood grew progressively bleaker as I trudged back to the car in my new, clomping corrective shoes—all the while rehearsing in my mind how unfair this life had become. "They were wrong to do this to me," I murmured to myself.

Ingratitude is ugly. We teach our children gratitude instead of entitlement because no one can tolerate a self-absorbed person. Looking back on it now, I can see what a brat I was. How hard could it possibly have been to muster up a tiny, two-word "thank you"? But I rebelled and, at that moment, could not bring myself to say anything good.

God Deserves Our Thanks

Doesn't God deserve our gratitude *far* more than any man with a piece of candy?

What has God given me, just today? When I woke up, the breath of life had pulsed in and out of my lungs all night long, rhythmically keeping me alive without me thinking about it at all. The sun, without me lifting a finger to sustain the planet, steadily rose over my house and yard, keeping my plants alive. I had a sturdy roof over my head. Unlike many times in the past, I even had air-conditioning. The plush bed under my back perfectly contributed to ideal sleep, both cushy and comfy. My head rested on a trove of hypoallergenic pillows meticulously collected by my wife. I had a ceiling fan moving cool air across my body, as if the central air-conditioning was not quite comforting enough.

When I emerged from my bedroom, every member of my family was healthy. I could move my arms and legs without knowing how I did it. I could take in the world around me with all five senses. I don't know how my sense of taste works, but when I put food in my mouth at breakfast, it tasted fabulous! I had clean water to drink, available at the turn of a little faucet, but I didn't bother to drink any of that. No, I made a whole pot of coffee instead, a drink that somehow wakes me up even though I have no idea how. And those are just physical blessings.

Throughout the day, I spent every moment surrounded by impenetrable angelic protection. The same Holy Spirit of God who hovered over the waters at Creation completely filled my body—offering moment by moment direction, even promising that one day I will stand forever under the loving gaze of the Father as He wipes away every tear and heals every ache of my soul. I awoke this day, like every other, knowing that I will one day celebrate eternally in heaven, each day better than the one before. On that day, endless, infinite time will amass effortlessly ahead of me. Every moment will pass with layer upon layer of pleasure and glory freely piling up, on and on forever.

In the face of all that, how could I ever forget to say a humble "thank you"?

Yet, instead of giving thanks to God for these many gifts, we often grow angry with God for the many things we wanted but did not get. Or we fuss about the gifts God *might* withhold from us in the future. Sometimes we fear that God might not protect us from future danger. It must madden Him to deal with our ugly ingratitude. He lavishes a cascade of gifts on us all day, every day, but we hungrily snatch them unnoticed. How much better would we navigate life if we consciously and regularly gave God thanks for all He continually does for us?

Cultivating a Lifestyle of Gratitude

God wills that we cultivate a lifestyle of gratitude; He wants thanksgiving to continually spill from our lips. Saying "thank you" puts our hearts in the right, humble place to hear from God. The Bible regularly tells us to thank God:

- "Tell God what you need, and *thank him for all he has done*" (Philippians 4:6, NLT).
- "And *give thanks for everything* to God" (Ephesians 5:20, NLT).
- "*Give thanks in all circumstances*; for this is God's will for you in Christ Jesus" (1 Thessalonians 5:18).

The whole of Psalm 136 is nothing but a list of miracles God has done for His people, the reminder that "His love endures forever," and the repeated command, "Give thanks to him!"

Adoration and thanksgiving are similar ideas in the memory device PROACTIVE. I have included both because they highlight two different but equally necessary practices.

Adoring or worshiping God emphasizes who He is: His nature and character and His great works that reveal His power. But *thanking* God emphasizes what He has done for each of us individually. The difference between adoration and thanksgiving can be illustrated by saying, "I worship and *adore* you, Lord, for who You are and for Your great acts of salvation for everyone; but I also *thank* You today for the kindness You have shown me personally by answering my prayers." Adoration is about who God is in general; thanksgiving is about what He has done for us specifically. Being thankful keeps our souls open to hearing from God. People who hear from God tend to be grateful people.

In the second chapter of the book of Daniel, the prophet asked God to reveal the Babylonian king's dream. That night Daniel saw the answer in a vision. He responded immediately with gratitude: "Praise the name of God forever and ever. . . . He reveals deep and mysterious things and knows what lies hidden in darkness. . . . *I thank and praise you*" (Daniel 2:20, 22-23, NLT).

Daniel's life teaches us that God reveals mysteries to people overflowing with gratitude. If Daniel had failed to thank God, would the revelations have continued? I'm not sure. But Daniel was a powerfully thankful man. In fact, Daniel got thrown into the lion's den specifically for his habit of thankfulness: "He prayed three times a day, just as he had always done, *giving thanks to his God*" (Daniel 6:10, NLT). Eventually, Daniel heard from God about the moment in history when the Messiah would come (Daniel 2:44 and 9:26). Daniel sets the example for us that gratitude plays a role in extraordinary hearing.

Daniel expressed his gratitude even in the tough times. Invaders had destroyed Jerusalem and dragged Daniel away into exile. He had to learn a new language and culture and soon began to serve his captors as an advisor. What exactly did he thank God for three times a day? Yet there he was, thanking God and receiving revelation.

What do you want that God hasn't yet given you? Can you give thanks for what you already have?

Learning Gratitude Again

We wanted babies. When Rebecca and I got married in 1989, we just knew we would have children. Doesn't everyone? For a while, we felt satisfied to live life as a young, carefree couple; but as our departure for the mission field drew near, an invisible emotional pressure began to build. We could feel our clock ticking, running out of time to have children in the safe, secure setting of our home culture.

Surely, it would be wiser to have babies in the US instead

of West Africa! God would do the wise thing, wouldn't He? In the country where we were to work in West Africa, we had no reliable blood supply to help in case of complications during birth. We both felt anxious about that.

About three years into our marriage, one doctor soberly told us that we could never have children. We cried often after that. It put a strain on our relationship with God. It tested our ability to be grateful.

By 1993, we were all prepared and trained up for the mission field. We had amassed a meager $24,000 a year in support. Since French was the governmental language in the country where we would move, we first headed to France to learn French. We knew this would be our last opportunity to have "safe" pregnancies.

And sure enough, while in France, Rebecca got pregnant. We bought several pregnancy tests: All came back positive. After what doctors had told us, we wanted to be absolutely sure.

I remember brightly chattering about our first pregnancy in front of a video camera, taping the news to send to our families back home. I doubt if any other footage we have ever taken could compare to the giddy joy we experienced taping that pregnancy announcement. I could not contain my rapture.

A week or two later, Rebecca and I visited a French hospital for an ultrasound. We nervously waited to see the baby's heartbeat as the lady squirted clear gel on Rebecca's slightly swollen tummy. The woman smeared a sensor around to miraculously reveal the interior of the womb. When I failed to observe what I expected to see in the grainy image, horrible doubt crept into my thoughts. A dark space in the womb appeared where the baby should be. We heard no heartbeat. We saw no tiny arms or legs gently curled up in a ball. Just darkness.

The ultrasound technician turned and spoke the most traumatic comment, just a few words that Rebecca and I can never forget: "*Pas de bébé.*"

I thought, *Did she just say, "No baby?"* As tears of disappointment silently rolled down our faces, the doctor came in and piled indifference on top of our devastation.

"Hey, it's not serious," he said. "Don't worry about it."

No one had warned us that a significant percentage of first pregnancies end in miscarriage. Gratitude to God was the furthest from our minds. We felt traumatized.

My feelings never plummeted so far, so fast. Fortunately, I had not yet sent that video announcement to our parents. Overwhelmed with the enormous gulf between our elation and the bitter reality, I carefully erased our joyful videotape so no one would ever see it. In the coming days, we suffered immeasurable, unimaginable grief and disappointment.

Those first years working for Jesus felt brutal. Rebecca's mother passed away during our year in France. We had an ectopic pregnancy not long after the miscarriage. Before long, Rebecca's father was diagnosed with lung cancer. Life had pretty much beaten us down to hopelessness. We had no expectation of having children by the time we headed to West Africa.

We moved into a village lacking any guarantees of safety. We lived in a small, tin-roofed shack with only bicycles to get around—no car. A single solar panel provided our electricity. Malaria-carrying mosquitos formed clouds around us. People often told us that having malaria during pregnancy puts the baby at mortal risk. A worse time to get pregnant could not exist.

Gratitude did not characterize our house. If anything, we felt angry at God. When we became missionaries to West

Africa, we accepted the truth that we might die. Many missionaries had. But we hoped He would shield us. We knew, however, that God is God. He made us, and ultimately only He decides when we return to Him.

That's what made us so mad at Him. We so desperately wanted Him to make our lives happy . . . and He had no obligation to do so.

Yet right there, in the midst of our first year of sincerely rugged village life, God gave us our first child. Oh, we went back to the States for four months to give birth to her, but we raised her in the village.

She soon grew into a four-wheel-drive toddler whom we could not contain. We constantly pursued her. If our backs turned for so much as an instant, she would dart through the screen door, barefoot and clad only in a diaper. She would sprint through the stickers to a nearby slope and scoot on her bottom down the rocky hillside trail leading into the village. As she scraped her diaper along the sharp stones on the steep gravel slope, she left a trail of tiny bits of absorbent white material that I used to track her movements and retrieve her. She learned to master a treacherous world.

Once she grew old enough to talk, she gave a tour to a group of visiting interns. They told us that she had gravely pointed out a deep, gaping, hand-dug hole in the ground and soberly warned, "That's a well. You could die. Really." Our second daughter was born equally rugged, running wild with her sister across the savannah.

When Rebecca became pregnant with our third child, the worst-case scenario finally happened. She fell ill with a severe case of malaria, pretty much maximizing the possibility of having another miscarriage. Of course, at the time I was a five hours' drive away on a mission trip and had to race across the country to get home.

I found Rebecca desperately feverish, lying on the floor of our bedroom, barricading the door by holding it shut with her feet to keep our two little daughters from evading her groggy care. My wife is a saint. No, I mean it. I think she need perform only the posthumous miracle and it's official. Our son survived and was born perfectly formed not long after that.

The doctor had told us we would never have kids, but we have three. Despite our lack of gratitude and trust in God, He proved Himself worthy of both. He proved His faithfulness!

All three of our children have had malaria, many times. They grew up just twenty miles from a bloody war. We could hear the artillery from our house. We have had to evacuate. We often dodged bouts of civil unrest and violence. Near misses while careening around mountain roadways became commonplace.

God didn't have to preserve our lives, but He did. He had no obligation. No one can tell Him what to do. That's the very reason I can never thank God enough for kindly answering our prayers for protection. If I ever let myself dwell on it, if I ever open the door to the full measure of emotion, the mountain of gratitude makes me tremble. It brings a messy, weeping, tearful thanksgiving from which I find it hard to recover.

When I think about how precious my adult children are to me, when I think of how close we have come to car wrecks and diseases, and yet we all remain alive, I feel overwhelmed. Tears leak out of my eyes. A sweet emotion rolls over my heart to think that my babies are in my life today only because God personally, graciously moved to give them to us and meticulously protected them from every harm, despite so much danger. I literally shake as I reflect on His bountiful providence.

Expand the Scope of Your Thankfulness

What has God given you? Think about it. Some obvious answers may quickly come to mind. But maybe, if you think a little longer, you can begin to widen the circle of blessings for which you feel truly grateful. Maybe you can gradually expand the scope of your thankfulness to God.

That's what I plan to invest a little time doing every day when I come to the *T* in PROACTIVE. Maybe I can grow my ability to deeply feel the intensity of true gratitude instead of that ugly sense of entitlement that comes so naturally to me. And maybe, as He did with Daniel, as I pour out my thanks to Him daily, God will choose to speak His mysteries to me.

Discussion Questions

1. Have you ever felt angry with God instead of thankful? Why?
2. How does wanting something you don't have make it hard for you to thank God for what you do have?
3. How do you react to people who receive your gifts and efforts with entitlement instead of gratitude?
4. What has God given you for which you feel the greatest gratitude?
5. If you are in a group, take turns practicing thankfulness by going around the circle, saying what you are grateful for. Say, "I thank God for __________ because

__________." (If you are alone, make a list of things for which you thank God.)

6. How do you think your gratitude to God might impact how you hear from God?

CHAPTER 10

INTERCEDE

We do not know what we ought to pray for, but the Spirit himself intercedes for us through wordless groans.

ROMANS 8:26

MY WEST AFRICAN FRIEND had problems. I don't mean first-world problems like figuring out how to stream Netflix on his smart TV. He had epilepsy that the local witch doctors had treated until he got so far under the influence of demons that he became a raving, uncontrollable menace. In his own words, he couldn't see human skin without trying to bite it.

He said that the sorcerers of the village had closed his throat. For twelve days, he couldn't swallow any water or food. Everyone around him just waited for him to finally quit screaming and die.

Meanwhile, back in the village where Rebecca and I were raising our family, we had just finished an eight-week sermon series about how Jesus gives us power to pray for the sick and cast out demons. For years, people in the church had believed that they were at the mercy of "the night people," sorcerers who learn satanic magical techniques that give their souls the power to leave their bodies at night and consume the souls of others, causing chronic disease or death. Our sermon series taught that Jesus has authority and power to oppose such evil spiritual powers.

The church began to pray powerfully for the sick and courageously cast out demons. At this time, only three toiling little churches existed among the Yalunka people on our side of the border. When folks from surrounding villages heard that a new source of power had become active in the Yalunka territory, they started coming from miles away for the church's help.

The church would passionately fast and pray, laying hands on the sick and crying out to God for healing. Couples with no children dejectedly approached the church and soon, after times of fasting and prayer, were granted the blessing of their first baby. One lady with debilitating headaches traveled from a village that was a forty-five-minute drive away. She left the church overjoyed.

I remember one man who trekked a several hours' drive away from a completely different culture because he had heard of a powerful medicine man in our village. When he arrived, people in town told him not to bother; the real power was available down at the church. I saw one man bring a sick child on the back of his motorcycle. Another man came because someone had stolen his cows.

These people don't always get their problems solved, but

the Christians pray fervently, and God often moves in great power among them. They have a reputation as powerful intercessors. The surrounding neighbors say, "When the Christians pray, God listens."

One day, I clambered up to the top of my baked-brick and cement-plastered water tank to clean out the algae and scum. As I hunched over inside the basin, grunting and scrubbing the accumulated filth off the walls that hold my drinking water, I heard a muffled voice calling me from below. I stood up and poked my head out the tank to find the church pastor down on the ground, asking to borrow my vehicle.

"I went to the next town over to see a friend I grew up with," he explained. "He was lying there, tormented by demons. He hadn't eaten for twelve days. When I walked in, he shouted, 'Jesus Christ has come to save me!' So can I borrow your car? I'm going to go get him."

Of course, I agreed. The pastor drove with four strong men to the neighboring village to collect his friend. On the way back, they held him down, keeping him from kicking out windows or escaping to run screaming off into the bush. Once they returned to our home village, they heaved him out of the car and deposited him in a weathered old hut next to the church.

As soon as they got him situated and prayed for him, he said, "You can let go of me now; I'm all right."

The Christians shook their heads vehemently. "No way."

He persisted: "No, seriously, you can stop holding me down now. I'm fine."

The pastor said, "Well, if you really *are* better, would you eat something?"

When I arrived to add my prayers to theirs, they were shoveling heaps of food into his wide-open mouth, baby-bird-fashion, using a huge spoon. I've never seen anyone eat mounds of rice like that. He guzzled water and grinned like he had never sipped anything so sweet.

So, of course, he started coming to church. He gradually regained his strength and began to learn to follow Jesus. He continued to need medical treatment for epilepsy, but he stayed in his right mind. He kept his spiritual freedom from demons.

One Sunday, the men of the church decided the time had come to celebrate this man's astonishing recovery. We returned to his village to hunt monkeys, also known as "tree deer." In West Africa, that's how we roll.

As the Toyota Land Cruiser pulled up to his hut in his hometown, he stepped out of the truck into his old neighborhood to a hushed silence. Dozens of people shyly surrounded us to peer at him and whisper. More than one finger furtively pointed as people leaned together, passing shocked queries back and forth. The last time they saw him, he was screaming, snarling, and snapping—nearly dead from thirst and out of his mind. Now, nothing appeared the same. He seemed healthy. He was going hunting.

I could see in their eyes one question: *Who is this Jesus that these Christians talk about? How does He have such power to answer prayer?*

Later, the man's wife would tell me their story like this: "I began following Jesus because He's done a miracle for me. When I came, I was anxious; I was running around everywhere. But today, praise God! We don't go to diviners, we don't worship idols, and we don't have magic medicines. We content ourselves with God, and we have peace."

Pray for Others

God answers intercessory prayer.

> Is anyone among you in trouble? Let them pray. . . . Is anyone among you sick? Let them call the elders of the church to pray over them and anoint them with oil in the name of the Lord. And the prayer offered in faith will make the sick person well; the Lord will raise them up. . . . The prayer of a righteous person is powerful and effective.
>
> JAMES 5:13-16

God intends for us to become people who intercede for everyone around us. Just like the Yalunka church, people should know us as righteous people devoted to powerful prayer, sought after for spiritual help by everyone around. For that to be true, we need to begin praying for those around us.

When someone comes to your office, do they leave without you praying for them? When someone visits your home, do they return home without anyone lifting up their needs? When someone confides in you, do you offer only advice, or do you also pray? Do your children know they can count on you to intercede effectively for their life problems? Do sick people regularly ask you for prayer?

After worshiping, confessing, and thanking God, we finally get to the part of the PROACTIVE memory device that seems a bit more intuitive. The *I* in PROACTIVE stands for intercession, lifting up the needs of others. Here we plead with God for Him to heal the sick or to give our children a career, a good spouse, and divine comfort. In intercession, we call out to God that He would bless us and those we love.

Moses powerfully exemplified this kind of intercession. "As long as Moses held up his hands, the Israelites were winning, but whenever he lowered his hands, the Amalekites were winning" (Exodus 17:11). Later again, Moses' powerful intercession proved crucial.

> Then once again I fell prostrate before the LORD for forty days and forty nights; I ate no bread and drank no water, because of all the sin you had committed, doing what was evil in the LORD's sight and so arousing his anger. . . . But again the LORD listened to me. And the LORD was angry enough with Aaron to destroy him, but at that time I prayed for Aaron too.
>
> DEUTERONOMY 9:18-20

Who in your life needs a person like Moses, asking for God to show them mercy and not wrath? Intercession can lead to hearing from God.

One day while I preached in Oklahoma, I met a lady who opened up about prayer. She had lived the Christian life for decades.

"I used to have a great prayer life," she told me. "God used to talk to me . . . and it wasn't always enjoyable. The first time He spoke to me was a scolding. But you have to have a good prayer life for God to talk to you. And now that I'm old, when I start to pray, my mind wanders."

This woman's experience seems similar to my own. I find that when I pray, God talks to me. *And* my mind wanders. She perceptively brought up the problem that keeps many of us from praying. We can't pray even for a few minutes without the worries and cares of this life intruding. People often tell me that they aren't good at prayer because their mind wanders.

If your mind roams, that doesn't necessarily mean you are bad at prayer. It may just mean that the Spirit is causing your mind to wander to show you what to pray about. Or maybe it's not the Spirit. We may get distracted by the "worries of this life" (Matthew 13:22), because Satan uses that as a trick to keep us from praying.

There is a solution. We can learn to pray *about* those distractions and worries. If you pray about worries, you might find that you have a lot to pray about! You could suddenly find yourself praying for an hour or more as you lift up to the Lord one concern after another. Talking to God for an hour about your troubles could be powerful because that's about the time that God starts to talk back, at least in my experience.

If you worry about your kids, your job, or your marriage, then pray about those things. We are such gifted worriers that prayer about our concerns can go on for a long time.

Organizing Your Prayers

I like to organize my prayer times using all the categories represented by the letters in PROACTIVE to help me keep everything in balance. Under the part labeled "Intercede," I carefully write down all my family members. I copy and paste a Scripture to guide my prayers for each child and for my wife.

I have a section where I pray through the Beatitudes for Rebecca and me: "Lord, help Rebecca and me to be poor in spirit so we will come to receive the Kingdom of Heaven. Help Rebecca and me to treat others gently so that we will inherit the earth. Bless us with hunger and thirst for right living, and satisfy us. Help us show mercy to one another and others in need so that You also will show us Your mercy. Make our hearts pure so that we will see You every day. Lord, help us build thriving communities at peace with You, so we will be called Your children." That's what I mean by "praying Scripture" for my family. I base my prayer on the words of Scripture, modified to match the situation of the people I'm praying for.

But I don't just pray Scripture; I also carefully write out my requests for each loved one. Remember, it matters more what you *pray* for someone than what you *do* for them, because God has infinite power and you don't. Even before they were born, I cried out to the Lord to bless each child. I begged Him to give me Kingdom-of-God babies. For two decades now, I have prayed, "Oh God, in some quiet moment, draw my children to your side and nurture their souls until they overflow with your Holy Spirit." I pray that they would each know God profoundly and that they would grow healthy, strong, and prosperous. I ask God to help them learn languages, to take on cleaning responsibilities around the house, to choose the work right for them, and to serve God in their career by fulfilling their created purpose.

I pray for my children with the unabashed bias of a daddy. I prayed for years that they would each make all A's in school. In fact, when I wrote *Extreme Prayer*, I used that "prayer for all A's" as an example of praying specific prayers. But those who helped me edit the book questioned the legitimacy of my example. Some wondered if that was a realistic, positive example of a prayer for one's children. What if they just can't do it?

Well, it certainly was true that my kids were not all making all A's when I started praying that they would. But that's kind of why I started praying. As a daddy, I wanted God to lavishly bless their academic work.

Still, I took the example out of the manuscript in deference to the input I'd received. But I kept it on my prayer list. That was back in 2013. Around four years later, I remember taking note that the unrealistic had come to pass. *All* my children were making all A's. That situation didn't last forever, but for a time, I could undoubtedly see that God had moved in great power.

Intercession is a huge blessing both for me as I pray and for the people I love and pray for. You might wonder, *Could just anyone pray for such things and see God do them? Does this always work?* I'll be honest: I have no idea. Why don't you try praying for something for four years and find out?

Intercessory Prayer and Extraordinary Hearing

Intercessory prayer plays a vital role in extraordinary hearing. As you pray through the list of people you love and make your requests for them, don't feel shocked if ideas start flowing into your mind. A sudden desire to call or text someone you are praying for may strike you. Or perhaps you'll find yourself reminded of something you forgot to do for your spouse. You may get an idea for advice you think might help your son or daughter.

I write down all of those on the back of my prayer list. Sometimes I take notes on my phone. I often sense these as God's marching orders for me, showing me how to be a good husband and father.

Would I hear such guidance from God if I didn't pray for those I love? I doubt it. Extraordinary hearing requires that you pray for the people you influence so that you get in a position to receive guidance and help from God to nurture them in a way that pleases Him. Godly people eventually learn to keep intercessory prayer as their go-to first step before anything else.

A Cry in the Night

One year as I slept peacefully in the early morning hours under my gauzy mosquito netting in my village home, my close friend and pastor, Paul Samura, who lived down the hill by the church, started to bleed internally—maybe from ulcers or from some parasitic infection. In Africa, we seldom get a clear diagnosis.

Paul's sister crept up to a window at the back of my house in a frenzied panic. She began clapping her hands and repeating my name in one of those shouted whispers that frantic people use to wake up someone unexpectedly in an emergency. I could tell from her stumbling rush back down the hill once I woke up that her brother must surely be near death.

I sprinted to Paul's house, where he lay on the bed like a dead man. One glance confirmed his critical condition. Then they showed me evidence that convinced me he had lost a lot of blood and had a very short time to live. I ran up the hill, leaped into our vehicle, and bumped and lurched down the trail, intent on rushing him to the hospital.

When I arrived with the car, we gathered around, leaned in, and began tugging at his limbs to move his limp form. Suddenly jerking conscious with a gasp, Paul shifted his head and groaned with all his strength, "Pray for me!" Everyone froze and exchanged stunned looks. Why didn't we think of that?

We pushed the pause button on my haphazard ambulance routine and gathered everyone around to intercede for him. Shadows, cast by several bobbing flashlights, shifted on the dark hut walls as we gently laid hands on him and cried out to God for mercy. Pleading voices echoed into the silence of the dark night sky.

Instantly, he looked a lot better. Of course, we loaded his slack form into the car and took him to the hospital. Upon our arrival, we dedicated more concentrated time to pray for him again. He looked steadily better all through the night. One church member stayed with him that night until dawn, begging God to spare his life.

Before you credit the hospital with his recovery, remember that this was Africa in the 1990s. They gave him two antacids and a vitamin K shot to help his blood clot. They didn't even run an IV to replace fluids or provide blood to replace what he had lost. I'm sure they helped. But I *saw* him improve instantaneously with my own eyes. The prayer of righteous people reversed the situation from certain death to inevitable recovery.

Paul recovered in that moment, but some years later, a similar crisis killed him. The lesson from this experience is not that God always heals the sick when we intercede. We might wish that were the case, but we know that everyone in this fallen creation eventually must die, except in the event of Jesus' return.

No, my point here is that Pastor Paul's stunning example of faith in God radically corrected my faulty worldview. I discovered that night that I still need to learn to go *first* to God, to trust the Creator more than modern medicine.

What if you found yourself in a similar situation? In a deadly crisis, would you stop the people rushing you to the hospital and demand prayer first? Yeah, me neither . . . yet. But I'm learning.

Pastor Paul had so profoundly internalized his knowledge of God that his gut instinct in the throes of death was to call out for intercessory prayer. I would have called for medicine. I might have shouted, "Get me to a doctor!" I can still hear the intensity of his voice, like a rebuke to my American perspective, begging instead, "Pray for me!" He really, *really* believed that God powerfully answers prayer. He would and did stake his life on it. Someday, I will get to take my final exam on faith. I hope I pass, like Pastor Paul did.

A Lasting Treasure

I still walk by Paul's house on my way to church when we visit West Africa. Before his death, Paul meticulously prepared every detail of the mud brick and conscientiously crafted the roof for his round hut with his own rough hands.

The thatched roof long ago rotted away. One year I walked by, and the basketlike woven bamboo cone of poles supporting the thatched roof had collapsed and crashed inside the house's mud-brick walls. The roofing materials eventually disappeared from within the walls, little by little, gently worn away to dust as wood bores and termites fed on them. The exposed mud walls have gradually eroded down to broken, curved arcs of melting rows of bricks that still memorialize the circle of Paul's house.

Much of what Paul built during his life has crumbled to dust. But he left us at least one enduring treasure. His example calls you and me to hide this truth deep in our hearts: *Intercession is more urgent than action because God has unlimited power.*

Discussion Questions

1. For whom do you think you should start interceding in your prayer life?

2. Have you ever tried praying Scripture for someone? If so, how did you find it helpful?

3. The Bible says in Exodus 17:11 that so long as Moses held up his hands (in prayer), the Israelites won. How do you think your intercession affects people's lives?

4. How will you make sure you remember to systematically lift up in prayer everyone under your influence and spiritual leadership?

5. How do you think interceding for the people you love will help you hear guidance from God about those people?

CHAPTER 11

VANQUISH

The Lord *said to Satan, "The* Lord *rebuke you, Satan! . . . Is not this man a burning stick snatched from the fire?"*

ZECHARIAH 3:2

P R O A C T I V E
a
n
q
u
i
s
h

THE BALDING MAN in dark pants and a long-sleeve shirt struck the passing hotel patrons as tall, but otherwise unremarkable. No hurried, frantic behavior tipped off anyone in the days leading up to October 1, 2017, in Las Vegas. The man pulled up to the hotel in an average minivan and asked hotel employees to move his heavy suitcases into his room.

After coolly and diligently preparing his thirty-second-floor suite, Stephen Paddock ruthlessly fired more than 1,100 rounds of ammunition into a crowd of people peacefully enjoying a concert. He killed fifty-eight people and left another 422 with bloody gunshot wounds.[15] More than four hundred others were injured in the blind, panicked stampede fleeing from beneath the murderous hail of gunfire. He wrought all that destruction in just ten minutes, then fatally shot himself without a word of explanation.

Do You Believe in Demons?

I used to think that Americans did not believe in demons. The scientific worldview teaches us that only what we can see and touch is real. So when something inexplicable happens, we say, "That's just your imagination" or "There must be some rational explanation." That's what we say so that no one will think we are crazy.

But that's not what we really believe: "Nearly seven-in-ten Americans (68 percent) believe that angels and demons are active in the world."[16] Of course we do. We can tell by looking at the world around us.

How else do you explain the Las Vegas shooting? What rationally explains the epidemic of public shootings in our culture? When I type the word "school" into Google, the third suggestion on Google's list of recommended searches is "school shooting." How did attacking children in school become so commonplace?

The rational, logical explanation is that Satan and his demons are real, indescribably evil, and move in our lives, trying to destroy us. Just watch the news. It would take a great deal of faith in science to explain our world today without ultimately agreeing with the biblical idea that evil, unseen powers are hard at work to block out any source of light. Paul says:

> For our struggle is not against flesh and blood, but against the rulers, against the authorities, against the

> powers of this dark world and against the spiritual forces of evil in the heavenly realms.
> EPHESIANS 6:12

What and where are these evil spiritual forces in heavenly places? Do *you* believe that demons are real? If you read the Bible, you probably have been convinced, at an intellectual level, to think they could be real. But do you believe it enough to take action in your daily life to fight them?

Your mother and father told you a long time before you read the Bible, "Monsters are not real." Why do we say this to our children? Why not teach them instead to be spiritual warriors? We need to learn how to fight and defeat demons.

If you remain skeptical, let me ask you this: Have you ever had an experience where you woke up in the middle of the night, terrified, and you didn't know why? I have met many people who had an experience like that. The simple explanation is that the Bible is right about unseen powers.

Unclean spirits really do attack people. Wouldn't you like to know how to kick those demons out of your house so that you never have to feel spiritually helpless again? God willing, by the end of this chapter, you will.

Where Demons Come From

I have concluded that Revelation 12 teaches us that one third of the angels rebelled against God and got kicked out of heaven: "Then another sign appeared in heaven: an enormous red dragon with seven heads and ten horns and seven crowns on its heads. Its tail swept *a third of the stars* out of the sky and flung them to the earth" (Revelation 12:3-4). The dragon represents Satan while the stars are angels. The spiritual war being fought on the earth started in heaven.

These former angels joined with Satan to fight against God:

> Then war broke out in heaven. Michael and his angels fought against the dragon, and the dragon and his angels fought back. But he was not strong enough, and they lost their place in heaven. The great dragon was hurled down—that ancient serpent called the devil, or Satan, who leads the whole world astray. He was hurled to the earth, and his angels with him.
>
> REVELATION 12:7-9

Now, filled with bitter hatred, these dark spirits relentlessly oppose us.

> "Woe to the earth and the sea, because the devil has gone down to you! He is filled with fury, because he knows that his time is short." . . . Then the dragon was enraged . . . and went off to wage war against . . . those who keep God's commands and hold fast their testimony about Jesus.
>
> REVELATION 12:12, 17

They want to hurt God, but they can't, so they attack people instead, trying to hurt God indirectly by turning his precious children against Him. If they can cause the people God created, His treasured kids, to suffer in hell with them, that's how they can hurt God the most. It is their highest prize.

But remember, they aren't like God. They have limits. The Bible teaches in the book of Job that Satan can't harm us without God's permission (Job 1:6-12), and we learn in Romans that God works all things—even demonic opposition—to the good of those who love Him (Romans 8:28). That makes

Satan the unwilling servant of God. He tries endlessly to hurt us. He designs his attacks of intimidation to discourage us, make us fearful, or turn our eyes to him. But God uses even the most spiteful attack for the good of those who love Him.

Demons Turn People Away from God

Demons' overarching goal remains the same no matter what part of the world they inhabit: to harm people or lead them away from God to their eternal destruction.

While I worked in West Africa, it amazed me how consistently the Bible explained the demonic experiences of the Yalunka people. One time as we shared the gospel in a village, I met a man who explained that he couldn't follow Jesus yet. "A spirit has loved me," he said, "and he promised to help me build a house. Later, I can follow Jesus." I often used to explain, "A demon loves people like a fisherman loves fish. He puts something delicious on the hook, but it's not out of kindness."

Another dark night in a distant village, a local evangelist and I taught about the Bible to a small crowd of fascinated people. Everyone had a copy of the book of Genesis that we gleefully read together. They had never seen any writing in their language before that day. The gospel had never been proclaimed in that place. An oddly behaving character came meandering by, looking at and handling every curve of my dusty Land Cruiser while talking to himself in three different voices. Sometimes his voice rang out in a shrill shout, then abruptly shifted, dropping down to a fairly normal voice. Then again, his voice would suddenly transform to a low, gravelly mutter.

I ignored him for a while and kept on teaching. But as he drifted a few paces away, he suddenly whirled around with his hand outstretched, jabbed a finger at the gathered crowd, and shouted the first intelligible thing I had heard him say: "Are you educated? Do you think you can read? I am telling you, Yalunka is a small language. Stop trying to learn to read it. Stop trying to read those books." People looked down in embarrassment at the outburst and began glancing at one another. To my astonishment, the crowd broke up and walked awkwardly away.

Demons will do anything within their significant but limited power to stop the preaching of the Word of God.

My Yalunka friends told me many stories of seeing and talking with demons, all explainable as demons drawing people from God. If these experiences with spirits were all just a figment of their imaginations, how would their stories so clearly line up with what the Bible predicts demons will do? These demons are real. They are equally active worldwide and have the same objectives.

Demons try to distract us from obeying God so we will follow them into hell. God made hell for them, but they, spitefully, don't fancy the idea of suffering alone in it.

I once thought demons were more visibly active in West Africa than in the West, but now I see they simply have different strategies for different cultures. In Africa, where people believe in them, they appear openly to scare the living daylights out of people and inspire them to worship them. But in the United States, people don't really believe in them, so they cleverly stay hidden. Why should demons appear before an atheist and prove that unseen powers exist?

Not the Whole Story

Along the way, I've learned this is not the whole story. One year at Oak Hills Church in my hometown of San Antonio, Texas, Max Lucado asked me to preach about Ephesians 6 and spiritual warfare for seven minutes at the end of one of his sermon series.

As I prepared the message, my six-year-old son sauntered in and asked, "Hey Dad, what are you going to preach?" I explained that I was preparing a talk about casting out demons. He turned to me with all the scientific sophistication a six-year-old can muster and bluntly commented, "Sounds a little crazy to me, Dad." He drew out the word "crazy" for emphasis, his little head nodding reassuringly all the while to soften the blow.

I glanced down again at the manuscript, as if seeing it for the first time. "Yes, Son," I mused aloud, "it does, at that." Right before the service, Max scanned my manuscript with a growing look of concern and said, "You'd better finish with a prayer after this."

For some listeners, I imagine that those seven minutes seemed like the weirdest in the history of the Oak Hills pulpit. Over the following week or two, people applied my teaching about how to cast demons out of their houses. One person reported back to me, "We had been struggling in our marriage and feeling oppressed in our home, but now it's all gone. We had thought we were losing our minds." I heard several stories like that.

I don't know how many people applied my teaching—maybe dozens, maybe hundreds—but I picture puzzled demons bouncing to the curb outside Christian homes all over the city. Years later, people continued to contact me with questions.

I know many Americans who have experienced something they don't understand, but they refuse to talk about it openly. That's why I now believe that demons are just as active in the United States. Some think their house is haunted by ghosts.

But the Bible teaches far more about demons; it barely mentions ghosts.

Why tolerate demons when we have the power to cast them out?

Demons may do the greatest damage when they magnify a secret sin in our lives. By harboring misdeeds in our hearts, we give them permission to have a foothold in our lives. When a demon targets us, temptation can spin out of control: Lust becomes an addiction to pornography, sickness becomes chronic disease, and conflict becomes bitter rivalry.

Don't Ignore Unseen Powers

We in the US have a tendency to pretend demons aren't doing anything to us. Explaining unseen demons to Americans sounds just like explaining unseen bacteria to a Yalunka villager.

I would sagely say, "You are sick because you have a bacterial infection." They would scrunch up their face and question, "What's that?" I would respond in professor mode: "Bacteria are living organisms so small that you can't see them." Then they would ask, of course, "Well, if it's so small, how can it hurt me?"

I imagine at this point my eyes would widen, taking on that maniacal look you get when you become a little too earnest in describing a danger. My hands would gesture widely about the room, indicating invisible threats all around. "There are millions of them!" I would exclaim. "They are on every surface!" Taking a baby step back, they would gaze at me with that gentle expression reserved for delusional people, remarking, "*E! Tubabune!*" which translates loosely as, "You poor white man, bless your heart."

Yet, I was right. There really *is* an unseen threat called

"bacteria." We Westerners all believe that, even though most of us have never seen one.

It's the same thing for the Yalunka people who have observed the dark side of the spiritual realm. They say they *have* seen demons. We could learn from them.

In this spiritual war, we are a bit like soldiers strolling through a battlefield with bullets whizzing and ricocheting about, bombs wrecking people's lives all around, and yet we refuse to fully engage the enemy. We look around in shock and question, "Whoa, how did the youth minister get addicted to porn?" Or "How did the church leadership end up in such a bitter conflict that it split the church?" Spiritual grenades detonate all around us, destroying lives, but we don't tend to clearly see the connection to spiritual warfare. No one could be more vulnerable than a soldier on the front lines who doesn't believe in the enemy.

Drive Out Demons

Paul teaches us to fight. He says:

> Therefore put on the full armor of God, so that when the day of evil comes, you may be able to *stand your ground*, and after you have done everything, to stand.
> EPHESIANS 6:13

Demons are as real and present in your everyday world as bacteria and can be just as deadly. The Bible instructs us to take a stand. The word translated "stand your ground" means to "stand against" or to "resist." Here Paul is referring specifically to resisting demonic forces. He's saying, "Stand up to demons."

Our knee-jerk reaction is to think we fight by praying to God, and that's important. But I have concluded that Paul means for us to do more than pray to God *about* demons. Talking *about* someone is not the same as taking action *against* them by resisting them. We are called to directly oppose them.

Two other biblical writers use the same word to teach the same idea:

1. James says, "*Resist* the devil, and he will flee from you" (James 4:7).
2. Peter says, "Your enemy the devil prowls around like a roaring lion looking for someone to devour. *Resist* him" (1 Peter 5:8-9).

One biblical model for "resisting" demons is to follow the example of Paul and Jesus by commanding them to leave. Acts tells about a young slave girl who, in the Greek, "had a python spirit," which our translations interpret as a spirit that helped her predict the future. A demon was influencing her. She followed Paul and his companions for days, shouting accurate public service announcements about them. Paul eventually had had enough: "Finally Paul became so annoyed that he turned around and said to the spirit, 'In the name of Jesus Christ I command you to come out of her!' At that moment the spirit left her" (Acts 16:18).

First, notice that the text doesn't say, "But Paul, covered in goosebumps and quivering in fear . . ." No, he was ticked off at this satanic influence in an innocent girl's life. We have no more reason to shrink back in fear from demons than Paul did.

Also notice that the demon left *only when Paul commanded it to leave.* That's the model that Paul and Jesus show us for how to "resist" demons. He didn't bow in prayer and ask God for help. Not right then. It wasn't time for that. Instead, he claimed Jesus' authority and kicked the spirit right out of the girl and away from his ministry.

Some people tell me that we should pray *instead* of casting out demons because Jesus once said, "This kind can come out only by prayer" (Mark 9:29). When I read that whole story, however, I see that the context supports both prayer *and* driving out demons. Jesus loudly commands the demon to leave. That's how we "resist" demons. We have no record of Him praying at the time He opposed the demon. He prayed in advance, before the battle. Jesus had just descended from a mountain prayer time. I believe He meant, "This kind can come out only by a powerful *lifestyle* of prayer." To win the fight, we need a PROACTIVE spiritual life. But demons do come out *when* we drive them out verbally in Jesus' authority.

Not Reserved for Apostles Only

Verbally casting out demons isn't something reserved only for the twelve apostles. In Luke 10, Jesus sent out a huge group of normal, everyday non-apostles to announce the Kingdom. Jesus confirmed that He had given these followers power to drive out demons in His name: "I have given you authority to trample on snakes and scorpions and to overcome all the power of the enemy; nothing will harm you" (Luke 10:19). These were just average folks who followed Jesus, and they commanded demons to leave in Jesus' name—even before the arrival of the Holy Spirit! How much more powerful are we whose very bodies are filled to the brim with the same Holy Spirit who hovered over the waters at creation?

Someone might object, "Just because Jesus and His followers did it doesn't mean we can." I believe Jesus taught that those who trust Him will do all that and more: "Whoever believes in me will do the works I have been doing, and they will do even greater things than these, because I am going to the Father" (John 14:12). We believe in Jesus too! So God has given us the authority to command demons to leave.

Jesus did it. Paul did it. Jesus' disciples did it. The demons are still at work today. Casting out demons is just one of the things we do in the Kingdom. The King has given His followers the example and the authority "to overcome all the power of the enemy" (Luke 10:19). Driving out demons verbally still works today.

Spiritual forces all around us can attack us, and unless we order them out, we may be letting them ramble about our home or our places of ministry. We need to follow Paul's example and order them to leave.

Do you do this? Many people don't. Maybe they feel "a little crazy," like my son said.

Years ago, I had a conflict with some colleagues. I felt angry, but I forgave them. Months later, I began to find myself repeatedly reminded of the conflict. I felt more and more bitter about it. I prayed nearly every day but praying by itself would not remove the bitterness. Finally, I cried out to God, "Lord, show me why this is happening to me!"

It was as though God lifted a curtain. I became aware of a demon intensifying those feelings of resentment. I said aloud, "*You* did this to me! I command you in Jesus' name: You leave me alone and go wherever Jesus sends you." The burden of bitterness suddenly lifted from me like a crushing weight. I'm not saying I was demon "possessed." *When the Spirit of God fills us, demons cannot also possess us.* But they can tempt us and influence us. The Bible says that demons harass you too. You can fight them!

Spiritual Warfare Maintenance

Sometimes when people become aware of the reality of spiritual warfare, *everything* becomes about that.

Other people become aware of spiritual warfare for a time and address it for a season of life, but then they lose track of it.

So in trying to keep a balanced, sustainable approach, I have compared spiritual warfare to changing the oil in my car. I don't have to change the oil in my car if I don't want to. And it will be fine . . . for a long time. Then the engine will blow up.

Spiritual warfare is similar. You can do without it just fine for a long time . . . and then your life blows up. I regularly use six tools in spiritual warfare. I practice them something like one to three times a week. Here are the six tools I use in spiritual warfare maintenance:

1. PUT ON GOD'S ARMOR

I spend time regularly praying for help to put on each piece of God's armor, but not as some kind of magical incantation. Instead, I like to reflect profoundly on the meaning of each armament. It fascinates me that the armor that defeats Satan isn't creepy, magical stuff like we see in the movies.

Like me, you may have "learned" a lot of dubious ideas about spiritual beings from years of watching scary movies. We need to unlearn and thoroughly erase from our minds every detail of Hollywood theology regarding unseen powers. Who do you think made up those movies? That's the devil's advertising department! The weapons that defeat Satan are not incense and spooky Latin incantations, as you see in films. The explosive spiritual power that roughly shoves aside the darkness turns out to be living the fundamentals of the Christian life.

Think about these words:

> So strap on all the weapons of God so that you can stand up to evil when it comes. And after you have overcome it all, you will still be left standing. Therefore, brace yourself by buckling *the belt of truth* around your waist and strapping *the breastplate of right living* on your chest. Lace up *the footgear of training* to spread the Good News that brings peace. Always keep your *shield of faith* up so you can snuff out all the flaming arrows that the evil one fires. Accept *the helmet of salvation* and *the Spirit's sword*, which is the message of God. And lift up every prayer and request in the Spirit moment by moment. Through it all, watch over all God's holy people in prayer. *Never stop praying.*
>
> EPHESIANS 6:13-18, GPT

Paul teaches us: Protect your core with truth. Cover your heart with right living. Train hard to race from place to place with the Good News that brings peace with God to everyone you meet. Block Satan's temptations with faith in God and a faithful life. Refute the thoughts the devil would insert into your mind by intimately knowing that you are saved and by listening to your Savior. Sharpen your knowledge of Scripture so the Spirit can use it to cut away Satan's strongholds in people's lives. Protect the backs of your fellow soldiers every day by covering them in prayer. That's how we fight with God's weapons!

Satan has been shooting at you. If you haven't properly armored up, then you've taken some hits from long, slender thorns sunk deep into your chest and side. You know where these injuries are; they're the places in your life that hurt. Sin hurts. Think about these wounds. Then think about yourself, and in repentance, gingerly remove each slender, painful spine from your body. Then, armor up. Think about how each weapon protects your vulnerable soul.

2. PRAY, "DELIVER US FROM EVIL"

Jesus taught us to pray for God to deliver us from evil. So, following the example of the prayer Jesus taught His disciples, I often pray, "Deliver us from evil" (Matthew 6:13, ESV). The way it's worded in the Greek language, it can mean either "deliver us from the evil one" or "deliver us from evil" in general. So I take the opportunity to pray against both.

The Bible talks about evil people, evil thoughts, evil spirits, and evil events, such as catastrophes. My regular prayers for my family include elaborating on the words of Jesus. We say, "Lord, deliver us from evil: evil people, evil thoughts, evil spirits, and evil events."

3. ASK GOD FOR ANGELS

The work of angels clearly includes taking care of us: "Are not all angels ministering spirits sent to serve those who will inherit salvation?" (Hebrews 1:14). For me, part of spiritual warfare includes asking God to send mighty angels to guard my home and family.

One day, I got a call from a friend in West Africa. He'd been sitting in a hut, dimly lit by lantern light, talking to a group of new believers. He called me from his cell phone to pose a theological question.

"The last several nights this lady has had a large, dark-colored bird come perch upon the pinnacle of her hut, calling out in a low, hooting cry," he began. "We all know that's a sign that the sorcerers of the village have targeted her and her family to eat their souls. What should I teach her from the Bible?"

At times, it seems like I'm still in seminary, periodically having to take theological pop quizzes.

Among other things, I reminded my friend to have this woman pray for God to send angels to protect her home. I searched on my computer for key Scriptures and read them aloud over the phone:

> I looked up and saw a man dressed in linen clothing, with a belt of pure gold around his waist. His body looked like a precious gem. His face flashed like lightning, and his eyes flamed like torches. His arms and feet shone like polished bronze, and his voice roared like a vast multitude of people. . . . Then I heard the man speak, and when I heard the sound of his voice, I fainted and lay there with my face to the ground.
>
> DANIEL 10:5-6, 9, NLT

"That's what angels look like," I explained. I took a moment to let that sink in. "If God sent one of these angels to protect you and your family," I queried, "would the sorcerers in your village be powerful enough to harm you?"

One resounding response echoed from the crowd of believers huddled together in the obscurity of that hut: "No way!"

When we put our kids to bed each night in West Africa, we rarely failed to pray, "Lord, post your angels around our home." Our three-year-old daughter tried it out one evening at bedtime. Tiny, pudgy hands fervently folded, forehead crinkled up in full focus, she lifted her adorable little voice to God: "Lord, toast your angels around this house." A long, silent pause interrupted her prayer as she thought, *That can't be right.* Using the intercessory backspace-delete function, she gave it another shot: "Lord, toss your angels around this home."

Then it was my turn to pause in silence while that mental image played out—angels flipping through the air and landing upright like water bottles casually pitched about by a divine hand. I'm sure our home was well protected one way or another! And my kids grew up knowing how to defend themselves from evil. It came in handy when they went off to college.

Ask God to send angels to guard you.

4. DEDICATE THE PLACES WHERE YOU LIVE AND MINISTER

Sometimes I walk around my house or workplace with my arms outstretched. "Lord," I say, "as surely as the Tabernacle and the Temple were set apart for holy purposes, so I dedicate this house for the gospel of Jesus as a place of worship for you." This resembles Jesus' teaching for His followers:

> Whenever you enter someone's home, first say, "May God's peace be on this house." If those who live there are peaceful, the blessing will stand; if they are not, the blessing will return to you.
>
> LUKE 10:5-6, NLT

Jesus believed in blessing and dedicating homes to be places of peace. He commanded His disciples to do that everywhere they traveled; so can we.[17]

So, I invite you to regularly dedicate your home as a place of peace, worship, and prayer.

5. DRIVE OUT DEMONS

Whenever I walk around, dedicating my house or office to God, I also take that opportunity to command demons to leave it in Jesus' name. I don't know if demons can hear what I'm thinking, so I speak *out loud*. I prefer to do that when my neighbors aren't watching.

Why don't you close this book and try it out? Say, "In the name of Jesus, I command you to get out of this house and go wherever Jesus sends you." Take a few minutes to practice saying those words out loud. Go say them around your house. Repeat them at your office. Get used to driving out demons you can't see. That's an important tool in spiritual warfare.

6. TURN AWAY FROM EVIL

One year, I learned from my Christian neighbor in West Africa the necessity of turning away from evil. He told a story about people coming to him for help to release a man who had been paralyzed by demons. He said he was able to release the man when no one else in the village could because "I don't know them, and they don't know me." My neighbor was saying, "I have no business with evil spirits, and they have no business with me."

That made me realize how important repentance is in spiritual warfare. I began to cast out demons, saying, "Get out of this house, in Jesus' name. I have nothing to do with you and you have nothing to do with me." Often when I would say that, a secret sin that I had been harboring in my life would pass through my mind. As if the demons were answering, "Ah, but you do. You have this sin in your life. That's the red carpet you rolled out for us." That reminds me just how crucial turning away from evil really is.

Then I say, "All right, as of right now, I am repenting of that sin. I'm not doing that again. So now, I have nothing to do with you and you have nothing to do with me. You get out, in Jesus' name." People often call this, "renouncing" evil in your life. I don't mean to say that we need to be sinless to drive out demons; but we do need to continually repent and turn away from our sins to be in a strong spiritual position.

Get rid of sin; it's like an engraved invitation for Satan and his demons.

Take Your Stand

Don't run around the battlefield barefoot in your gym shorts and a T-shirt. Take full advantage of all the weapons God gives you to fight! Try these six tools for spiritual warfare maintenance:

1. Put on the armor of God.
2. Pray "Deliver us from evil": thoughts, people, spirits, and catastrophes.
3. Ask God to send angels to guard your home and family.
4. Dedicate your home as a place of worship and prayer.
5. Regularly drive demons out of your home and workplace.
6. Turn away from evil in your life.

One year, a family living near our office was preparing to go overseas. Their young son kept having breathing problems that forced the family to rush the child to the emergency room. It terrified both them and us. We began to face the fact that, if these episodes continued, this family could not go overseas.

One day, I wondered, *What if this is a spiritual attack?* On my way home, I swung by to visit the family. I sat down in their living room and taught them about spiritual warfare maintenance tools. They said they would try it.

The child never had to visit the emergency room again for that problem, so far as I know. The family went overseas.

Don't let demons hang around. What demonic attacks are you needlessly tolerating? Why let them turn temptations into addiction, conflict into bitter fights, or sickness into death? Instead, "take your stand against the devil's schemes" (Ephesians 6:11) and run them off in Jesus' name. Imagine what your life can be like when they are gone. How much more clearly might you hear from God without them?

Discussion Questions

1. What do you believe about demons?
2. How do you think unseen spirits may be impacting your life right now?
3. What experiences have you had with unseen powers?
4. How have you practiced spiritual warfare in the past?
5. How do you think casting demons out of your life might affect how you hear from God?
6. How do you plan to implement spiritual warfare maintenance in your life? How often?

CHAPTER 12

EXTREME PRAYER

Son of man, watch and listen. Pay close attention to everything I show you.

EZEKIEL 40:4, NLT

P R O A C T I V E
x
t
r
e
m
e

DO YOU EVER struggle to know what God *really* wants you to do?

I wrestled with a moment like that one morning in June 2017. I needed God to tell me whether He wanted Pioneer Bible Translators to launch a major initiative to start translating the Bible into the sign languages of the world for the Deaf.[18]

As a Bible translator, I had been quite surprised to learn that, in addition to the almost 7,000 spoken languages among the hearing, around 400 sign languages also are used by more than 70 million Deaf people in the world.[19] Who knew? I sure didn't.

Once we became aware, we made some efforts to help

with sign language translation; but by June 2017, we had not yet fully committed. I knew that I needed to get involved somehow, but I saw two main possibilities. I could raise some money and send it to those mission organizations who already used their gifts to work among the Deaf. Or I could transform our organization to begin working on our own sign language Bible translation projects.

The first option seemed both safe and easy. Most people I asked thought that just raising money for partnering organizations would be the smart path. We probably wouldn't do a lot; our specialty has never been fundraising. But it would be enough to make me feel good, as though I had contributed *something*.

The second option would radically upend our well-oiled organizational machine. I had begun to feel convinced that we should choose the second option because I now grasped the vast scope of the work among the Deaf. Our partners needed *a lot* of help to get the job done. A symbolic gesture would not be nearly enough. The Bible translation movement needed more people and resources efficiently invested in the sign languages to catch up with the spoken languages.

But which choice was God's will? I really needed to *know* from God what to do!

I began getting ready to develop a fundraising appeal to our whole investor community, publicly saying that we would recruit, train, and send out Deaf missionaries to go to the Deaf worldwide. I knew that once I made such a statement, we could not turn back. But without God's power and blessing, I feared it would turn into a spectacular train wreck, with me blowing the whistle the whole way.

So I sat down at my desk and prayed. I started simply enough: "God, I really *need* to know. Should we get personally involved in sign language Bible translation?" And then I listened. I cocked my head to the right with my left ear pointing upward, straining my senses—as if my *ear* would hear the reply. At first, I got only profound silence.

Then, after repeating the question several times, I had one of the most unique experiences of my prayer life. Without an audible voice, God clearly impressed upon my mind the thought that He *absolutely* expected us to get involved in translating the Bible into sign languages. He also emphatically communicated that He was *angry* with the Church for marginalizing and neglecting the Deaf.

I started my prayer time sitting casually at my desk, but by the end, I was down on my knees, shuddering a little in awe before God's expression of wrath. It reminded me again of what God said to Jeremiah: "'Does not my word burn like fire?' says the LORD. 'Is it not like a mighty hammer that smashes a rock to pieces?'" (Jeremiah 23:29, NLT). It sure felt like a hammer. It burned too.

I had begun my leadership journey as if Jesus had died only for hearing people. This experience in June 2017 made me fully repent of ignoring the Deaf. I've left behind half-hearted measures. Now, it's personal.

But I still had a niggling question about what God showed me. Why would God be so angry about something like that? I didn't understand.

Why So Angry?

A couple of months later, some staff members from Deaf Missions[20] came to visit our office. Most of them are Deaf. Hesitantly, I told them my story about hearing from God that He was angry at the Church for ignoring the Deaf. It was a risk.

I couldn't know how Deaf people would react to a story like that from a hearing person. They have been marginalized by hearing people their whole lives. I didn't know much about Deaf culture, and I didn't know whether my words would offend them.

But as I told them of my experience, a subtle shift took place in the room. Several had tears welling up in their eyes. Some of their faces looked more intense than before. Finally, one man said, "I'm glad to know that God is angry about that. I've been angry about that for a very long time."

After interacting with them about their point of view, I began to understand why God's message had not made sense to me. Part of it wasn't *for me*. I hadn't understood because I didn't really know Deaf people. But that day, as I watched their faces glowing as they prayed in our prayer tower, something changed in me. I could see that these people are God's precious children. Of course, He would be angry. He gave us the message of life to share with everyone, everywhere—not just the hearing. And we have not yet been diligent using the sign languages of the earth to make disciples. Not yet!

What if you told your son that your daughter was in danger and sent him to go save her life? And what if, hours later, you found him playing around instead? Wouldn't you be angry? Our situation is not much different. Jesus commanded His followers to make disciples of *all* nations, including Deaf people. But if God had been counting on me to share Jesus with any Deaf people, they sure didn't get the gospel from my first few decades of service.

Not long after our friends' visit, I joined the board of Deaf Missions and started pouring more of Pioneer Bible Translators' organizational energy into recruiting, training, and sending Deaf missionaries to the Deaf.

Pray about God's Own Passions

My story illustrates the last habit needed to cultivate our hearts for extraordinary hearing. We must learn how to pray about things that God Himself is passionate about. Otherwise, why should we expect Him to give us specific directions?

If many of my prayers concern my own comfort, convenience, and wealth, it might turn out that God has little interest and no guidance to give me about such things. He might think that getting more comfort and money would devastate my spiritual health. God may seem utterly silent because we haven't yet asked Him any interesting questions.

When we pray about ushering in the justice of God's Kingdom to our neighborhoods or the world, we may find we have finally attracted His full interest. He may have *a lot* to say. Prayer is not about getting whatever we want. It's how God releases His power in us to get whatever *He* wants.

Extreme prayer is not the same as intercession (at least, not in the way I'm using these terms). In intercession, we pray about things that *we* care deeply about, and rightfully so. But in extreme prayer, we pray about things that *God* cares deeply about, such as the advancement of His Kingdom.

The book of James teaches that intercessory prayer has power in part because *the person praying* is righteous. James wrote, "The earnest prayer of a righteous person has great power and produces wonderful results" (James 5:16, NLT). Our intercession for the things dear to us has limited power because our righteousness has limits. But extreme prayer brings unlimited power because the righteousness of Jesus has no limit. Jesus promised infinite power for this kind of prayer, so that's why I call it extreme prayer.

For example, Jesus promised unlimited power when we pray "in Jesus' name":

> Very truly I tell you, whoever believes in me will do the works I have been doing, and they will do even greater things than these, because I am going to the Father. And I will do whatever you ask *in my name,* so that the Father may be glorified in the Son. You may ask me for anything *in my name*, and I will do it.
>
> JOHN 14:12-14

In the Bible, names have meaning; they represent the character of the person. And Jesus' name means salvation. When we make requests consistent with His character, name, and mission, and under His authority, He answers with immeasurable impact. As you pray these kinds of prayers, you will attract the fervor of your heavenly Father and begin to hear His Holy Spirit.

The key to extreme prayer is to stop praying about our strategies and make prayer *the* strategy for accomplishing what God directs us to do. As we learn to organize our whole lives and ministries around praying the kinds of prayers that Jesus promises to answer with infinite power, we see God move in our lives as never before. Consider the biblical principles of extreme prayer:

- God answers prayer in Jesus' name (John 14:11-14).
- God answers persistent prayer (Luke 11:9-10).
- God answers unified group prayer (Matthew 18:19).
- God answers specific prayers that build our faith (Matthew 17:20).

- God answers prayers of faith and faithfulness (Mark 11:24).

When we place these principles at the core of our lives and ministries, we can experience the infinite power Jesus promised. Consider some steps for implementing these principles:

1. Ask God to show you what He wants you to do.
2. Listen for God's assignment.
3. Keep specific, strategic prayer request lists for the people you influence and the work of God's Kingdom around you so you can persist in prayer.
4. Regularly gather a group of people for unified group prayer.
5. Pray expectantly. Keep a pen handy to write down ideas and instructions you get from God as you pray.
6. Act on those marching orders you receive.
7. Watch for extremely powerful answers to prayer.

But how do you listen for God's assignment? You can find the answer in the outline of this book: First, understand how God spoke to His people in the Bible (chapters 1 and 2); next, cultivate a listening heart by developing a PROACTIVE devotional life (chapters 3 through 12); and then, learn through experience to discern God's voice (chapters 13 and 14).

Develop a Biblical, Group-Owned Vision

Some churches and ministries can't apply these principles because they don't have a group-owned direction from God that they try to accomplish together.

Ministries that lack clear, group-owned, God-ordained

goals cannot powerfully access the extreme prayer principles. Why not? Because the group doesn't know what to pray.

But once a group has finished the hard work of corporately determining Kingdom-oriented goals, they can make those goals into specific prayer requests.

Let's take the example of the illumiNations alliance in the Bible translation movement. This is an alliance of eleven large Bible translation agencies that have rallied around four goals called the "All Access Goals."[21] The illumiNations alliance envisions all people having access to God's Word by 2033.

- 95 percent will have access to a full Bible (all languages over 500,000 speakers).
- 99.96 percent will have access to a New Testament (all languages over 5,000 speakers).
- 100 percent will have access to at least some portion of Scripture.
- 100 of the world's most strategic written languages will be available in two viable translations.

While the work that went into the development of the goals must have felt daunting, just think about the power that has become accessible to those involved. They can transform each goal into a prayer. "Lord, please help us in the illumiNations alliance and your Church . . .

- to translate the whole Bible for all languages with more than 500,000 speakers by 2033,
- to translate the New Testament for every viable language with more than 5,000 speakers by 2033,

- to translate twenty-five chapters of Scripture for every viable language with less than 5,000 speakers by 2033, and
- to ensure that the top 100 languages of the world have at least two powerful translations of the Bible."

This alliance can experience the unlimited power Jesus promised when we pray according to all the principles of extreme prayer listed previously.

- The goals resonate with the name and character of Jesus (John 14:11-14).
- Clearly listing the requests empowers persistent prayer (Luke 11:9-10).
- Eleven Bible agencies are gathering in unified group prayer (Matthew 18:19).
- The specific requests build our faith (Matthew 17:20).
- The requests demonstrate amazing faith and faithfulness (Mark 11:24).

Jesus promised that these kinds of prayers transform the impossible into the inevitable. God Himself is so passionate about this kind of prayer that He will begin to speak to His body, and people will begin to experience extraordinary hearing as God teaches them how to become part of the answer to their prayers.

So, what about your church, small group, or ministry? Do you have a clearly articulated, group-owned vision? Have you turned that vision into specific prayer requests?

If you have no strategic goals, then begin there. Start by reading the Bible together and praying for God's guidance. Carefully scrutinize Jesus' life to learn His values. Then look around. A fire may burn in your soul as you see something in the world that Scripture teaches absolutely must change! Talk about that challenge in your group. Formulate some goals that you want to accomplish together. Once you have these goals, make them into your strategic prayer request list.

Make a Strategic Prayer Request List

My experience tells me that we can't release the full power of these extreme prayer principles without developing a strategic prayer request list. When Jesus taught that God answers specific, persistent, unified group prayer, He made it important for us to have a system. Persistent prayer seems simple: just keep praying the same thing.

But people need help remembering what we all are supposed to be praying. How can we get a large group of people all praying the same things, over and over, without a list of prayer requests they can all see? If we aren't recording specific requests, how will we even notice that God is answering our prayers? We might not see Him moving in power because we forget what we've been praying.

Many good systems exist. If you are artistically inclined, you can draw or make a prayer collage. If you are musical, you can pray while you play music. If you are physically athletic, you can build a prayer pattern into your workout routine.

Those are all good for individuals, but one fundamental method seems inescapable if you want to apply the principles of extreme prayer *in a group*: the prayer list. In a context where most people can read, it's the easiest way to align everyone around praying the same strategic requests.

Yes, I know that prayer lists can be used in a boring way.

But you don't have to murmur your way through it every morning. You can creatively divide it by day of the week or figure out other ways to spice up the way you pray. A list that includes world-shaking requests doesn't have to be dull.

Watching God shake up the world should excite us! If you don't want a boring prayer list, then don't pray boring stuff.

Pray Specifically

The number one obstacle stopping groups from faithfully praying a strategic prayer request list is the reluctance to pray specifically. It feels weird to have a list of specific things to pray, over and over again. We aren't accustomed to it.

Understand that when you first implement a strategic prayer request list, it will not come naturally. People will say, "Are we issuing ultimatums to God?" Praying specifically won't be a feel-good process at first; but if you keep going, you will eventually build a culture of prayer that strengthens the faith of everyone involved.

As you plan and create your list, establish only a handful of requests that rise to the level of needing everyone in your whole church or ministry to repeat them regularly in prayer. Choose carefully! Put these at the top of the page under the label "Strategic Prayer Requests." *This* is what you are crying out to God for power to do.

Then, I recommend that you insert a Scripture below the major requests to guide you in thinking about what comes next on the page:

> So Jesus answered them, "Trust God! I'm telling you absolutely that if you say to this mountain, 'May God pick you up and toss you into the ocean,' and if you

aren't a skeptic in your heart, but rather you trust that what you say will happen, then it will."

MARK 11:22-23, GPT

After the requests, make a list of the "mountains" that stand in your way. These are all the obstacles that seem to make the requests impossible. If God has indeed spoken and given you a mission, inevitably you will find that you don't have what you need to do it. You'll need people and money. You might not have the facilities. You'll lack the necessary skills and knowledge.

Specifically identify what stands in your way. If you need $5 million to build a facility, put down something like: "Lord, give us $5 million for the new building by the end of the year." If your church is searching for a new lead pastor, write something like: "Lord, bring us the right new lead pastor to take us into the future You plan for us, before December." If you need spiritual unity, write, "Lord, please help our team have perfect unity." If you need more small group leaders, be specific: "Lord, please provide seven wise and discerning small group leaders who are gifted disciple makers, by August of next year." When you finish, it should look something like the excerpt from Pioneer Bible Translators' strategic prayer request list on page 185.

In the whole process of extreme prayer, praying for God to move the mountains and obstacles feels the least natural. I've heard people say, "I just don't feel comfortable praying for numbers." Don't forget that a whole book of the Bible is called Numbers—so numbers can't be unspiritual to God. The numbers just identify which mountain needs to be moved and how big it is.

I've heard people object, "I feel like we are ordering God

Strategic Prayer Requests

- Lord, may we and our partners see churches with Scripture transforming every language community on Earth by 2050.

So Jesus answered them, "Trust God! I'm telling you absolutely that if you say to this mountain, 'May God pick you up and toss you into the ocean,' and if you aren't a skeptic in your heart, but rather you trust that what you say will happen, then it will."

MARK 11:22-23, GPT

Mountains

- God, please move our number of projects from 102 to at least 130 by 2024.
- Please help our team have perfect unity and growing ethnic diversity so that the world may believe that Jesus is for everyone.
- God, move your people to give $4.5 million for our next building and $3 million for sign language translations by 2024.

around." It may feel like that, but we are doing only what God has told us to do. Having the Scripture right there in the list helps to orient people around the reason we pray so specifically. These mountains stand between us and the God-ordained, biblically based, group-owned vision that we are striving to accomplish. We align all our work activities to accomplish this undertaking, consistent with the name and character of Jesus, and these obstacles hinder us.

Also, notice that not every specific obstacle in the example is numeric. You can definitely tell when God is giving you "perfect unity." You can also tell when you don't have it. It's specific, but it's not a number.

Years ago, a church I know had a campaign to raise $15 million. I attended one of its powerful vision-casting sessions. At the end of the session, everyone lined up to pray for the campaign. The prayers truly moved us as each person, one at a time, came up to the microphone. But I noticed one thing consistently missing: No one prayed for money. We all probably felt that praying for money would be unspiritual. And yet, a major objective of the campaign was to raise the required resources to implement the church's white-hot vision for Jesus in their community and around the world!

There comes a time in service to God when we should pray specifically: "God, please give us $15 million." Then, when God moves the mountains, everyone will grow in faith.

PROACTIVE Prayer Template

My experience says that God will not give me influence over anything I cannot support in prayer. The more powerfully my system of praying bolsters the people around me, the greater my spiritual influence and leadership grows. Just like Moses lifting up his hands in support of Joshua in the battle against the Amalekites (Exodus 17:9-13), so leaders must lift up what they lead. If you want to love and minister to more people, then you must become skilled at praying.

The best way I have found to make sure I stay steady in my prayer walk is to create a tool on paper that prompts me to balance my spiritual life, drawing on all the elements of the PROACTIVE memory aid. Enter pioneerbible.org/proactive prayer in your web browser or just search the internet for the "PROACTIVE Prayer Template." I have posted a document by that name that should make it easy for you to build your own prayer tool. Download that document to your computer and use it to design a prayer request list structured according to the memory device PROACTIVE described in chapters 3 through 12.

I like to use that template to develop my ideal set of prayer subjects under the PROACTIVE categories. Under the *PRO* part, I plan the spiritual patterns of my day and record insights from Scripture. I put some worship Scriptures under the *adoration* part to give me a little help worshiping. I leave space under *C* for confession. I leave space under *T* to write what I am thankful for.

The meat of the system starts with *intercession*. There I list the people in my family and the specific things I'm praying for each one. I paste in a special Scripture for each of my family members to guide my prayers. Under the *vanquish* part of the template, I have listed the six spiritual warfare maintenance tools. Then, under *extreme prayer*, I include my strategic prayer request list.

Organizing my prayers around a PROACTIVE system helps me stay balanced and support a much broader team in prayer. If you prefer journaling, you can structure pages of your journal with each of these elements.

God Answers Extreme Prayers

Jesus said:

> I no longer call you servants, because a servant does not know his master's business. Instead, I have called you friends, for everything that I learned from my Father I have made known to you. You did not choose me, but I chose you and appointed you so that you might go and bear fruit—fruit that will last—and so that *whatever you ask in my name* the Father will give you.
>
> JOHN 15:15-16

Jesus promised that as we discover the Master's business for us, He will choose us to accomplish that business and help us learn to get it done. As we orient ourselves around producing the eternal fruit that God has chosen for us, and as we learn to cry out to God, He absolutely promises to answer our prayers with unlimited power. That's how extreme prayer and extraordinary hearing come together—hearing from God what to do and praying to God for power to do it.

God will answer these kinds of prayers for anyone. No matter who you are, no matter how rich or poor, spiritual or unspiritual, God will hear you pray, and He will show you what He wants you to do.

The FBI Should Use It

One year I left my home in West Africa to take some time to reconnect with churches in the United States. During my absence from Africa, a band of thieves began stealing solar panels. They stole the panels off of the hospital. They pilfered the panels from the governor's mansion. They even had the gall to rob the panels right off the police station itself! Every solar panel for miles around vanished. And of course, the thieves eventually made their way to my village home, where they plundered the panels off of my house.

Church members were furious. "No way are these thieves going to get away with stealing Jesus' solar panels!" they said. So they got together regularly to fast and pray that they could catch the thieves.

Now, let's be realistic. How on earth can you catch thieves by fasting and praying? If you could, wouldn't the FBI restructure itself, with special agents in charge of fasting and prayer? But the Yalunka church trusted God.

One night, they held a special catch-the-thieves prayer meeting to break a daylong catch-the-thieves fast. Then, they sauntered out of the church and began to chat and argue, as Christians do the world over. And there, in the darkness of the roadway that passed by the church, lurked a man furtively walking by in the shadows.

One church leader dramatically pointed and announced, "That's the guy." Everyone said, "Oh, come on. You are saying that only because we just finished a special catch-the-thieves fasting and prayer session." He kept pointing and insisting that, somehow, he just *knew* the man strolling down the road in the darkness was the very thief they had just prayed to catch.

So the church members sidled up alongside the man and

confronted him. They asked some discerning questions and immediately noticed how nervous the man seemed. Then they caught him in an obvious lie. They searched him and found wires and wire cutters in his pocket. They took him to the village chief, who tied him up and interrogated him further.

The man admitted he was part of the rampaging gang of solar panel thieves. He had come to the village to slip away with the last solar panels in the whole region, those owned by a church leader working on the translation project. The thief knew they would be busy praying.

Then the church took him into town to the police. They soon found out that the thieves were reselling the panels in a city two hours' drive south. They took a police officer in a taxi to that city and cruised around town, confiscating stolen solar panels.

I had lost eight panels and I got eight panels back—and some of them were actually mine!

A pastor in town stood up at a huge meeting and testified that, out of all the panels looted, even from the police, only the people praying in Jesus' name got theirs back. The leaders of the whole region learned that God answers persistent, unified, group prayer in Jesus' name! Now nobody steals from that church anymore.

A few years ago, the church began regularly fasting and praying together for God to help them evangelize their own people. They now teach people how to follow Jesus in around twenty villages, spread over two countries and in three different language communities. We pray that they would plant a church in every major Yalunka village and then multiply beyond into the surrounding people groups.

If God can use His prayerful, spiritually receptive people to do all of that among people who follow the Quran in West

Africa, what is impossible for God? Nothing. Absolutely nothing is impossible for God.

Discussion Questions

1. Has God shown you a mission that He wants you to achieve in the coming years? If so, how did He make that clear to you?
2. How do you think praying about the coming of the Kingdom of God could help you hear from God?
3. What would you put on a strategic prayer request list for your church or ministry?
4. What specific mountains or obstacles do you need God to move out of the way so you can achieve your goals?
5. Download the PROACTIVE Prayer Template at pioneerbible.org/proactiveprayer (or search the internet for it). Then think through each area represented by the memory aid.
6. If you are working through these questions in a group, share with each other what you put under each part of the tool.
7. How might that template help you maintain a balanced spiritual life?

PART 3

EXTRAORDINARY HEARING

CHAPTER 13

PRINCIPLES FOR HEARING

Ask me and I will tell you remarkable secrets.

JEREMIAH 33:3, NLT

WHEN REBECCA WAS in high school, many young men at a Christian summer camp came forward to give their lives to "full-time Christian service," while the girls publicly committed their lives to becoming a preacher's wife. Something about that scenario just didn't sit right with Rebecca. Couldn't God lead a woman into full-time service too?

But in what work could she invest her life for Jesus? This young woman wanted a meaning for *her* life, not merely a meaning she derived from some random man she hadn't yet met. At one point, she took a bold step to ask a minister named Mark Worley what a woman who likes languages could do with her life to serve God. He said she could translate the Bible with Pioneer Bible Translators.

When she found out that women were freely allowed to participate, Rebecca plunged into a commitment to Bible translation like a falcon snatching prey. She felt in her bones that she was born to a life of godly purpose, and she could not be dissuaded. She wanted to please God above all else.

It came at a high personal cost. She became convinced that no man would ever come along who would willingly go into Bible translation with her and live for decades in remote areas of the world where she had decided to make her home. She concluded that God had called her to go alone, without a husband. She spent the summer praying for guidance from God and mourning all the things she would leave behind—husband, children, and family—by following Jesus into this specific future.

And then she met me.

God had worked in my heart too. I had decided in the ninth grade that I should become a missionary. As I went to college, I reflected that God could best use my skills if I became a civil engineer doing construction on the mission field. I didn't have a laser focus like Rebecca did, not until I heard that, among Muslims, there was only one gospel messenger for every million people. I thought, *If I were a Muslim open to hearing the gospel in a city of a million people in the Islamic world, what would be my chances of hearing about Jesus?* That question pierced my soul.

I devoted myself to that great sea of need, planning to share the love of Jesus with Muslims while working as a civil engineer (which would give me a way to enter countries otherwise difficult to reach). So God set the scene for an irresistible force to meet an immovable object. The resulting explosion became the great romance of my life.

Oh, I had met other girls who seemed intrigued by the idea of missions—or at least, open to it—but Rebecca remained

Gibraltar-solid in her resolve not only to go into missions but to become a Bible translator. Her unwavering commitment caught my attention and eventually convinced me that she was the girl for me. I admired her unshakable tenacity. It made me think that she would have the grit needed to work in difficult countries with me for the long term.

With enormous effort, I just barely managed to attract her gaze long enough to persuade her to go on a few dates with me. I became interested in spending my life with her almost right away. Those flashing blue eyes and passion for the Lord captivated me. I wanted Rebecca for my wife with as much passion as she had stubbornness and direction.

But we had a major crisis: a crucial need to hear from the Lord. Was it the Lord's will for us to pursue our relationship? We had to know. Our whole lives hinged on it. I contended that we should just go for it. I thought it would work out fine because, after all, we both were committed to missions and that should be enough. Surely, she could flex a tiny bit and do what *I* wanted to do.

She asserted with a stone-cold look that she would never give up her calling from the Lord for some hairy-legged boy. Okay, I might have embellished that last part, but the sentiment was unmistakable. I had never met such a resolute woman of character. It intrigued me all the more. I fell in love *hard*.

That didn't solve our problem, however. We attended various mission conferences together, every time playing out the same story. We would start talking about the future, and Rebecca would dump me. Three times she let me down hard! I clearly remember one breakup on a frosty day at the Urbana 1987 missions conference. There I met Rondal Smith for the first time, the president of Pioneer Bible Translators at the time. What rich situational irony! I didn't know that twenty years later I would become his successor as president of the very organization I then refused to join.

Rebecca and I had a significant problem. I wanted to work among Muslims, and Rebecca didn't believe Bible translation could be done among Muslims. We had a friend who worked in North Africa. He wrote letters home, telling about moving from town to town, distributing gospel tracts, and always staying one step ahead of the authorities. Rebecca just couldn't see how Bible translation could work like that.

I finally surrendered the fight in 1988 at a training event called Pioneer Missions Institute in Joplin, Missouri, at Ozark Christian College. Rebecca and I began to repeat the same old pattern of breaking up, when at last I changed my mind and decided I would join Pioneer Bible Translators with her. We would go wherever she wanted to go to do Bible translation. I would be a community development worker on her Bible translation project. I loved her that much.

At that point, we met one of our future mentors. He had joined Pioneer Bible Translators and founded our West Africa Branch in 1988. We felt overjoyed to hear that he was doing Bible translation among Muslims, exactly what we both wanted to do. "If he can do it," we said, "so can we!" I could share Christ's love with Muslims, and Rebecca could translate the Bible!

At that moment, we finally saw the path God had prepared for us. "If nothing else happens," we said, "let's just get married and go do that." That's how God taught me five principles for having extraordinary hearing.

1. Join What God Is Doing

What you hear from God aligns with what you see God doing. The first principle of extraordinary hearing overlaps with what many have learned in *The Purpose Driven Life* by Rick Warren. But that's no surprise because the teaching comes from Jesus in the Gospel of John. If you want to learn to hear from God, you must learn to imitate Jesus and these two teachings:

1. Assume God is at work around you.
2. Do only what you see God doing.

Jesus crystalized the first part of this principle for us when He said, "My Father is always working, and so am I" (John 5:17, NLT). Look at the world around you with the absolute certainty that God is always at His work. You have the opportunity to work with Him.

The second teaching builds on the first: "I tell you the truth, the Son can do nothing by himself. He does only what he sees the Father doing. Whatever the Father does, the Son also does" (John 5:19, NLT). Jesus refused to take any action except exactly what He could see God doing. What would your life become if you were able to see God at work?

I want this efficiency and power in my life. I want to be so in tune with the leading of the Holy Spirit that I can look out at the world and see exactly what the Father is doing, and then have the privilege and undeniable power of doing it with Him. One person alone can't do much, but any person plus God is already an unstoppable team.

So how can you see what the Father is doing? It will be something that only He could do. You look around your life and watch for a pattern in which several factors and a variety of unconnected people in your life all seem to come together to point in one direction, creating circumstances that only God could orchestrate for His purposes.

Take the example of Rebecca and me. She wanted to be a

Bible translator, and I wanted to work among Muslims, doing something with my engineering. We looked out at the world around us, and there, at just the right moment, appeared our future mentor, working on Bible translation among Muslims—both of our passions in one ministry. Not only that, but he also dug wells to meet the physical needs of the people. We saw that God had brought together in one place all three things that interested us: Bible translation, sharing Christ's love with Muslims, and engineering projects.

It looked like a strategy, but *we* hadn't strategized it. Only God could do that! We looked at the situation and said, "Hey, this looks like it's planned perfectly, but not by us. Let's go ahead and assume that this is God's will for us until something proves otherwise." We got married on that basis! And astonishingly, it worked. We translated the whole Bible and have been planting churches ever since. And the marriage turned out fabulous too.

One key principle in extraordinary hearing is to keep your hearing and your seeing synchronized. God's speaking will match what you see Him doing. Do what you see the Father doing—something that only He could do.

2. God Speaks through Your Created Purpose

What you hear from God aligns with your created purpose. Ask yourself, "What am I for? What did God create me to do?" You are *for* something. Assume you have a created purpose and search it out, based on this Scripture: "For we are God's handiwork, created in Christ Jesus to do good works, which God prepared in advance for us to do" (Ephesians 2:10).

The word translated "handiwork" is related to the English word "poem," a simple word that means "to do." It highlights the profound truth that God *made* us. We are God's poem, His masterpiece. We didn't just happen. He handcrafted us—our abilities, our circumstances, our experiences—all with pride and all for a divine, artful purpose.

Consider another way to translate that verse:

> For we are *His* masterpiece, created in Jesus, God's Anointed, for good works, which God prepared beforehand so *that we might walk in them.*
>
> EPHESIANS 2:10, GPT

Your life may seem out of control. You may feel useless and cast adrift in a dark world. But that's *not* the truth the Bible teaches! No, *you* are God's poem for a purpose. He made you with unique skills and abilities to do some good works in the world—and He prepared those good works "beforehand." Before you were ever saved or before the world was created, it's all the same to Him. Just "before."

God has prepared these good works for you to "walk in them." He stretches good works out like a connect-the-dots path ahead of you, traced out in advance. Do you want God's guidance? Look up! Do you see that good work placed out there in front of you *that you are uniquely able to do*? That's it! That is God's will for your life.

Hearing from God isn't a game of fastball where you keep swinging and missing as God pitches curveballs, all the while chuckling at your ineptitude. It's more like Little League tee ball that some of us played as kids. We stand there with our baseball bat resting lazily on our shoulder, while God perches that ball in front of us, setting it enticingly on the tee. Then He points at it and says, "There it is, kid; knock it out of the park." Yet it's still up to us to swing with all our might and keep swinging if we miss.

The key question is, What are you *for*? Look up ahead of you. What good work do you see that only God could prepare ahead of you, something for which you are specially created and shaped to accomplish? Are you alert? Are you looking?

He didn't say He would show you the ultimate destination; just that He would prepare works ahead of you for you to walk in. He shows you the next work on the pathway, but not where He'll ultimately lead you. When you take the first step, you can start to see the second one. After you take that one, He will show you another one. Eventually, you might look up farther, connect the dots, and see that, indeed, your road really has been planned out and stretched out in front of you by your loving Creator.

When Rebecca and I chose our work, it was based a lot on how we perceived our gifts and abilities. She thought she was created to work on translation, and I thought I was created to share Christ's love with Muslims. Then we looked up, and there we saw a man doing both of those things and asking for help. The work God had stretched out in front of us for us to do became obvious, but we never could have guessed where it ultimately would take us.

The business world commonly applies a similar idea, to base your career on your strengths. Marcus Buckingham[22] says that you should engage your strengths. He describes your strengths as the things that, when you do them, make you feel strong. What have you done that made you feel strong? What seems easy for you that others can't do? What fills you with passion, energy, and motivation?

Your giftedness is a form of leading from your Creator. The Bible says:

> There are different kinds of gifts, but the same Spirit distributes them. . . . All these are the work of one and the same Spirit, and he distributes them to each one, *just as he determines.*
>
> 1 CORINTHIANS 12:4, 11

God Himself chose the things you can do, and it matters not if the world sees them as flashy and important or if in your eyes they seem insignificant. God handcrafted you for something He has prepared for you to do! What are you *for*?

3. *When God Speaks, Move!*

Listening may seem passive, but it's not. What you hear from God will inspire motion. It's hard to lead a passive person.

I've met some people who paralyze themselves. They think that God must tell them everything first, and *then* they will become willing to step out in faith. But not until God clearly defines the whole road from start to finish!

Some people say that God has called them to the mission field, but they never act on it. They are just "waiting on the Lord." I can't imagine a way they would actually get to the mission field, because they won't take any concrete action to move in that direction.

Some people get the impression that all you have to do is say yes to God and He will whisk you away to the mission field or hand you a preaching position in a church without any effort on your part. Not so. Serving God takes disciplined, careful, proactive, intelligent, hard work on your part. You must *do* something to act on what He shows you. After all, He does call them "good *works*." A lot of work is involved!

One year in college, I went door knocking to share the gospel in San Antonio. A guy opened one door and said, "Oh hey, we are Christians too! We were in Nebraska and the Lord called us and told us to move to San Antonio, Texas." It blew me away. Here were people God had called specifically to help my hometown, by name. A desire to cooperate with their ministry suddenly seized me.

"So, what are you doing here?" I asked.

"Whatever God tells us," he replied. A silence stretched between us as I reflected on his answer, which gave me no content. I tried again.

"Okay, but what *is* it? I mean, what are you *doing*?"

"Just anything He says." The lack of clarity continued.

I peered over his shoulder and caught the impression of a whole house full of people milling around, apparently lacking any direction. In my youth, I may have judged too hastily; but from his answers, so far as I could discern, they were just hanging out inside this house.

Perplexed, I inwardly mused with more than a little sarcasm, *Thank goodness you got here in time.*

Clarity of direction is priceless! What do you know for sure about what God wants in your life? Has He made anything *at all* clear to you? If so, that's precious information. Even if you don't know everything, take bold action on what you do know. Do *something*! It's easier to guide someone who is moving than someone who's lying down.

Have you ever taken a kid by the hand to go clothes shopping, only to have the child go completely limp and tearfully crumple to the floor? You can't guide that child. You are left with the options of carrying, dragging, or leaving them behind; but you won't be able to lead them anywhere at all. Don't do that to God!

On the other hand, if a child starts toddling along with you, you can take them by the hand and lead them anywhere they need to go. In the same way, when we discover God's direction in anything, no matter how minor, we need to get up, take God's hand, and get moving!

4. *God Won't Hide His Will*

Even if you seem to hear nothing, God will not hide His will from you. When you need to make a decision about God's direction for your life, fast and pray. Spend time listening in prayer. Read the Bible. Reflect on what Jesus' life reveals to you. Ask God for guidance. Diligently take into account the whole process described in this book. Carefully weigh whether your decision will lead your life in an unscriptural or unhealthy direction. Invest a week, a weekend, a month, or a year, depending on the gravity of the choice.

But you can't put off deciding forever! You may not hear specific guidance from the Lord about everything. When circumstances dictate that you take action, do your best to perceive the leading of the Spirit and then move forward with confidence. In my experience, what you decide *will* turn out to be God's will—at least for that moment in your life. It's your responsibility to seek and His responsibility to reveal Himself to you.

God told Jeremiah, "You will seek me and find me when you seek me with all your heart" (Jeremiah 29:13). Once you have done your spiritual due diligence on some decision, take bold action in the direction that seems most right to you. If somehow you take a misstep, God will make that clear to you too.

5. *God Speaks to Christ's Body*

We need to learn to let God speak to the whole body of Christ instead of saying as individuals, "God told me . . ." What we hear from God individually should never close the door to the possibility that the Spirit is leading the whole body of Christ differently than we expect.

Saying "God told me" should not be taken lightly. How you explain your spiritual experience of direction from God is important to God. At a certain point in Israel's history, people falsely claimed to speak the word of the Lord. So God forbade people to even claim such a thing: "If any prophet, priest, or anyone else says, 'I have a prophecy from the LORD,' I will punish that person along with his entire family" (Jeremiah 23:34, NLT). God went on to explain,

> You should keep asking each other, "What is the LORD's answer?" or "What is the LORD saying?" But stop using this phrase, "prophecy from the LORD." For people are using it to give authority to their own ideas, turning upside down the words of our God, the living God, the LORD of Heaven's Armies.
>
> JEREMIAH 23:35-36, NLT

He's telling them to stop claiming unequivocally that they know what God is saying when they aren't truly sure. False prophecy is always punished in the Bible. So be careful about telling everyone, "God told me this" and "God told me that."

If you have often said, "God told me," with a degree of inflexibility implied in the statement, others may find you hard to work with. Someone who thinks of themselves as having continual, independent, and individual access to

God's will may not feel motivated to listen to the rest of the body.

That doesn't resemble how the New Testament Church perceived the will of God. In the church at Antioch, for example, Paul didn't say, "God told me to head to Cyprus." No, five people are mentioned by name, all fasting and praying together to perceive God's direction:

> Now in the church at Antioch there were prophets and teachers: Barnabas, Simeon called Niger, Lucius of Cyrene, Manaen . . . and Saul. While they were worshiping the Lord and fasting, the Holy Spirit said, "Set apart for me Barnabas and Saul for the work to which I have called them."
>
> ACTS 13:1-2

Notice that the Lord didn't tell them where to go. He just said *who* and *what*. Then they came to a consensus that they should go to Cyprus. God left them room to experience the leading of the Holy Spirit along the way as they sought Him and discussed God's guidance together, the whole body of Christ receiving the leadership of Christ, the head of the body.

In my experience, when people frequently say, "God told me" without leaving room for the input of the rest of the body of Christ, it doesn't work out in the end. The law of Moses commands Israel to stone anyone who presumes to speak on God's behalf whose prediction doesn't pan out (Deuteronomy 18:20-22). I'm not saying we should make stoning people church policy. I am saying that we should be careful how we speak about God's leading to avoid acting like false prophets.

When I sense the guidance of the Holy Spirit, I simply say, "In my prayers lately, God seems to be influencing me in this way . . . Does that match what you have perceived as you seek His will?" Then it becomes possible for God to instruct the whole body together. As with the church at Antioch, I find that the guidance God gives the group tends to be better than guidance I receive individually.

Sometimes we can't be sure. Paul talks about his leading from God at one point by saying, "And now, compelled *by the Spirit*, I am going to Jerusalem, not knowing what will happen to me there. I only know that in every city the Holy Spirit warns me that prison and hardships are facing me" (Acts 20:22-23). Luke writes that the believers at Tyre opposed this idea by the same Spirit: "*Through the Spirit* they urged Paul not to go on to Jerusalem" (Acts 21:4). Who heard best? Some confusion is natural as the invisible Holy Spirit works among flawed human beings. That's why I'm learning to proceed with some caution in my words.

Hearing from God is not merely a question of a whispered voice dimly perceived inside the mind. It must also align with solid biblical principles.

1. Join what God is doing.
2. God speaks through your created purpose.
3. When God speaks, move!
4. God won't hide His will.
5. God speaks to Christ's Body.

These extraordinary hearing principles will steer us away from common problems as we begin to strain our ears listening for God's voice. As we let God guide our lives and show us His will, we end up with the ability to fulfill our created purpose.

More than You Can Ask or Imagine

At the beginning of this chapter, I described how God worked to bring Rebecca and me together to do Bible translation among Muslims. But that's not all God had in mind.

We got married in my last year of college. Then we went off to Fuller Theological Seminary to prepare for the ministry. We chose Fuller because it had specializations in working among Muslims, community development, and Bible translation—everything we had interest in doing. Right after graduation, I flew out to Southern California and papered the town with résumés, trying to get a job. By the end of the week, one civil engineering consulting firm called and asked me to start work on Monday. We loaded up and moved.

One day, while Rebecca did her Bible translation classwork, I looked over her shoulder . . . and curiosity seized me. I asked her to sign me up for one of her classes, just so I could understand her work. I'm not sure how it happened after that. I was working thirty-five hours a week as an engineer and taking a full graduate course load, so I can't remember much, but one thing led to another. When I left Fuller Seminary, I was a Bible translator.

I had thought I would plant churches, but it turned out I was a translator. I learn languages compulsively. I love Greek and Hebrew. I became a really good Bible translator, and I loved it! My whole life is now dedicated to making sure that everyone, everywhere, has Scripture they can understand.

Imagine what I would have missed had I not met Rebecca and fallen so hard for her. If not for her, I would have overlooked my fundamental, created purpose.

But our God is always at His work. He knew how to lead us to our purpose. And these same principles of extraordinary hearing will keep you on the path to discovering your purpose and God's future for you too.

Discussion Questions

1. What is your created purpose and how are you fulfilling it?
2. What do you see the Father doing in your life and how are you cooperating?
3. When have you had a hard time deciding what God's will is for your life? What did you do about it?
4. How can we talk about how God is leading us individually and still leave room for God to lead our whole community together?
5. What's the very next action that God has made clear for you in your life?

CHAPTER 14

HEARING VOICES

Come to me with your ears wide open. Listen, and you will find life.

ISAIAH 55:3, NLT

MARIE FELT A nudge from the Lord that their business was called to "double." Her husband, David, put it in more earthy terms. "Marie had the word *double* in her guts," he said.

David and Marie had long received divine nudges about what God wanted for their business. For five years they had said to each other, "I have this inner sense that we should do this . . ." But they weren't sure what to do with those ideas that they felt came from the Lord.

In September 2017, David and Marie Hazell invited me to hold an Extreme Prayer retreat with the staff of their business, My Father's World.[23] They built this homeschool curriculum business when they returned from the mission field so that they could financially support Bible translation projects with their profits. I enthusiastically looked forward to having a prayer retreat with them. We planned to dream together about how to make prayer *the* strategy of their business and promote a growing culture of prayer among employees.

I started the retreat by covering the principles of extreme prayer (see chapter 12). I then told the story of how God had moved in power at Pioneer Bible Translators as we gathered in unified groups to persistently pray in the name of Jesus.

Marie is no newbie to prayer and ministry. She puts together the spiritual content of the Journey Every Day website.[24] She's spent her life reading the Bible to know and obey God. She has invested a lifetime cultivating the soil of her heart, little by little, every day. Marie has plunged herself deeply into an undertaking that God Himself has great passion for—Bible translation. She's a great example of what I'm talking about in this book; she has placed herself in the ideal position to walk with God and hear Him speak.

Marie later explained how God spoke the word "double" to her:

> I was super-charged by reading an email or blog post saying that prayer *is* the strategy. I loved it and pounced on that thought: *That is it!* Then, as you were doing the seminar, you described the growth of Pioneer Bible Translators based on prayer—and something inside of me got really passionate.
>
> At the break, I just went to David and said, "I want to double." That thought consumed me, coming from my deepest heart. *If we double*, I thought, *all this stuff for the Kingdom can happen*. I want to be that

> much more effective because there is so much need in the world. I just want to see God's Word go out.
>
> Because I felt it so suddenly and so passionately, I call that "God put it on my heart." It's a God-birthed passion. I didn't feel like it was coming from me. I felt like it was coming from something deep inside me, like God's Spirit or my spirit. It wasn't like I sat down and thought it up. I don't know why it was "double" and not "triple." To me, it felt like I was one with God's heart when I was saying that. God was sharing His heart with me and what He wanted to do through me. And we just had to have the faith to walk it out. It was the strength of the passion that made it clear to me. It totally overtook me. I would do anything to see that doubling happen.

I think Marie and the prophet Jeremiah experienced the word of the Lord in the same way: "'Is not my word like fire,' declares the LORD, 'and like a hammer that breaks a rock in pieces?'" (Jeremiah 23:29). It's no accident that you've seen that text pop up several times in this book.

At one break, right before the moment we created the strategic prayer request list for their business, Marie told David that she felt God was calling them to double.

When I hold a retreat for a group like this, one part seems to make the biggest practical difference: the part where we set up an easel and work on the first draft of the strategic prayer request list. I remember the pungent smell of markers on flip charts and people throwing out ideas as I scribbled them in my wobbly handwriting on the big white pad of paper. We got animated as we pointed and asked questions like:

- Could we make this one more specific?
- How will we be able to tell if God answers that one?
- How many of these are we asking God for?
- Should we say what kind we are looking for?
- By what time do we want God to do that?
- Is that really a God-sized prayer request?
- Is that going to turn out to be so pretentious that it's inconsistent with the character of God?
- If God answered that, would we be ready?[25]

Those kinds of questions flew around the room until we began to get a sense of developing consensus. All the ideas God had been birthing in their souls over the previous five years came spilling out onto the tablet. The whole staff contributed.

Finally, we came to a moment where I could sense that David, the company's owner, had a list formed in his mind. He would spend time by himself over the next few weeks prayerfully honing it.

That's one key spiritual role of the leader. Everyone participates, but a good leader synthesizes the ideas of the group into powerful words that become the group-owned vision. A leader prioritizes and clarifies the best ideas and then crafts the words that paint the future. The leader decides what the community will pray for toward that vision. The strategic prayer request list therefore must ultimately reflect the spiritual vision of the leader.

But it needs to be group-owned too. Everyone must see their fingerprints on the end product. The leader who casts vision alone prays alone.

When we finished, I stepped back to take in the list, marveling at one particularly bold request: "Double the impact by 2020." When we talk about a business, doubling the impact typically starts with doubling the client base. God would have to double the number of customers to answer that prayer.

Or so we thought.

In every fledgling prayer movement, a moment comes when God's people must choose faith over doubt. It takes a lot of trust in God to get your whole staff praying something bold like doubling in three years! What if everyone prays for years and you don't double? Wouldn't that embarrass you, not to mention God? Sometimes we shrink back right at this moment. We flinch and make general prayer requests instead, such as, "O God, please bless our impact."

The team could have objected to bold, specific prayer requests like this one. Someone in the marketing department could have grown nervous. I mean, who does everyone look at while praying that the client base will double?

Sometimes the leader must gently reassure team members: "We aren't praying to you. We are praying to God for Him to *miraculously* double our impact. This isn't on you; it's on Him." I wonder what those first staff prayer meetings were like back in 2017 when people started to say, out loud, "God, double our impact by 2020."

David and Marie and the staff at My Father's World did indeed begin praying together for God to grant their requests. They prayed specific, unified group prayers, persistently lifting up to the Lord the very request God had shown them they should pray. Somewhere in the unseen realms, gears started to move, spiritual momentum began to shift, and the first answers to prayer began with a trickle, then a flood.

But their customer base didn't double. In fact, all through 2018 and 2019, their clientele *declined.*

But radical shifts did begin to occur. One day, David excitedly sent me a video of people in Papua New Guinea carrying

My Father's World curriculum in ponderous sacks slung over their foreheads as they pushed through a thigh-deep, swift current to serve a school meeting on the other side of a river. His voice over the phone would rise in intensity and animation as he excitedly told me about schools in South Africa and Liberia using his homeschool curriculum.

The next thing I knew, Marie was making an English as a Second Language curriculum based on their homeschool materials that people started using in Honduras. David took trips to central Asian nations where Christ is not known, training people how to start businesses that minister in other countries.

We all realized that, when we asked God to double our impact, He might not think about impact the way we do. We all wanted more money for more Kingdom impact. But God showed no interest in the financial aspects of "impact." Instead, He just transformed their business into a worldwide mission—because nothing can stop Him.

If you give God the keys to your business and really and truly listen for His guidance, don't feel shocked when He punches the accelerator and drives your business all over the world!

That's what He was telling Marie: "I have twice as much spiritual impact in mind for you than you have yet dreamed. Go ahead and ask me to double your business. Just wait and see what will happen!"

It was not necessarily a financial doubling, but their spiritual footprint went from North America to worldwide.

Unleash His Power in You

Prayer is not how you get what you want from God. Prayer is how God unleashes power in you to get what He wants.

David and Marie's experience of having God speak to them often happens to others. In one survey, the Pew Research Center documented that 28 percent of US adults said that they talk to God and God talks to them.[26]

Our problem isn't that we can't hear God's voice in our head. Often the trouble is that we have *too many* voices in our head. We don't know how to tell if one of them might turn out to be a whisper of guidance from the Holy Spirit. We can't reliably tell the difference between our internal monologue and God's voice.

The fact that we have internal voices is not in dispute. According to a psychology research project about "inner speaking," based on thirty years of research at the University of Nevada, people experience inner speaking, on average, 23 percent of the time. Some people never reported inner speaking and some always did.[27]

People reported inner seeing and mental images too. Occasionally, people described inner speech as "just happening." Words came into their minds, but they didn't feel as though they controlled these thoughts. It's part of the human experience to have voices in our minds.

Why would we doubt that God could use that experience to communicate His own messages into our minds? The God who created the complexity of the human brain should also be able to speak words and thrust images into our minds. Isn't that how the prophets described hearing the word of the Lord? Sometimes God spoke words; at other times, He showed them pictures. Remember all those examples we mentioned from the Bible in chapters 1 and 2?

Luke mentions no audible sound when describing Simeon's experience of receiving messages from God:

> The Holy Spirit was upon him and had revealed to him that he would not die until he had seen the Lord's Messiah. That day the Spirit led him to the Temple.
>
> LUKE 2:25-27, NLT

How did the Holy Spirit reveal that information to Simeon? Such a detailed idea! How did He lead him to the Temple? Such a specific location! Did Simeon hear an audible voice? Or was it more like God using Simeon's "inner speaking" to put the message into his mind? Since Luke uses an abstract word like "revealed," I lean toward the view that Simeon experienced the voice of God in his mind, what I call extraordinary hearing.

Other Voices

How easy if every voice in our mind originated with either our own thoughts or a divine message! But those aren't the only two influences impacting our thoughts. Human influences from our family and the universe of media also surround us. Human expectations can intrude regularly into our minds. Some ideas that occur to us may come from our upbringing or from a media influence forming as words in our brains.

A major part of temptation includes demons confusing our thoughts, introducing ideas of their own. It was Rebecca who first convinced me that we need to guard against demonic thoughts. Back in our early years, she believed that all the thoughts in her head were her own. She felt she needed to be true to herself and take seriously every idea in her inner monologue.

One day, she found herself thinking, *I hate Greg*. Later, she felt perplexed when she thought back on it objectively. "Where did that come from?" she asked herself. "I don't hate my husband." Then she went to a teaching event at church and became persuaded that sometimes demons speak their message into our minds. Remembering that hateful phrase running through her head earlier, the teaching resonated.

Over the years, that idea has seemed to reliably help explain what people go through when tempted. Today, we both teach that we need to apply discernment to the thoughts in our head to evaluate their source. Satan and his demons can suggest evil ideas, but we don't have to accept them.

The internal influences I experience in my own spiritual life seem to have four primary sources: (1) my own thoughts, (2) the voice of human expectations, (3) demonic thoughts, and (4) God's voice.

Recognizing Voices

Our problem doesn't seem to be that we can't hear from God. It's not a lack of voices. Our problem is having too many influences, a host of voices running through our minds and not enough discernment. We haven't worked hard enough yet to test the voices and identify them. So how can we tell the difference?

Start by recognizing the impact the voices have on your life. We will know the tree by its fruit.

Sometimes you may find yourself overwhelmed with insecurity about whether you measure up to the people around you. Those thoughts may remind you of a person you know, and they may resemble the pressure you feel from your mother or father or friends.

- "Wow, are you going to *stay* this fat?"
- "How can you stand this much dust on the coffee table?"
- "You really need to mow the lawn."

These are merely the voices of human expectations. Harmless, right? Watch out when you try to please people, though! The apostle Paul said, "If pleasing people were my goal, I would not be Christ's servant" (Galatians 1:10, NLT). You will soon find that a major part of serving Christ includes deliberately deciding *not* to please people.

At other times, we find ideas that accuse or tempt. I'm sure we have all heard such voices crowding our minds:

- "I can't believe she said that to you!"
- "Here's what you should have said back."
- "What do you think he *really* meant by those nice things he said?"
- "A real Christian would just keep on fasting."
- "If it feels this good, it can't be wrong."
- "You will never change."
- "God couldn't really love a person like you."
- "Why even try to repent at this point?"
- "You have no reason to go on living."

That's not you. Only demons divide, tempt, accuse, and destroy. Never listen to those voices!

Yet again, during other moments, we may encounter a gentle nudge or a still, small voice. God's voice leads us to bear eternal fruit. His whisper leads us to a sense of satisfaction and peace and to a life well-led:

- "You have enough beauty in your life. You don't need to look elsewhere for satisfaction."
- "Go tell that person about my love."
- "Give generously to the poor."

- "Sell everything you own, pack up your family, and move to Asia."

When thoughts begin to enter your mind and you want to learn which ones are of the Lord, the following chart can help you:

SOURCE OF THOUGHTS	RESULT
You	Normal life at best and confusion at worst
Human expectations	Anxieties
Demons	Accusations, temptations, addictions, divisions, threats
God	Eternal fruit, peace, contentment, rest

Look at the chart and ask yourself, "When I acted on that thought, what was the result?" If your actions threw your life into confusion and perplexed the people around you, then you probably acted on your own impulses and impressions—thoughts that originated from the synapses of your own brain. You can rest assured that you are entertaining human ideas and not a message from God.

If you listened to a thought in your mind that led you to take action that bore eternal fruit, however, that's the voice of God. No other could do that. The voice of the Lord will lead you to a fruitful, sustainable life, full of peace, contentment, and rest. The voice of God will challenge you to achieve hard or even impossible tasks, but ultimately they will be hard in a healthy way, like lifting weights or running a mile. They will not be hard in a destructive way, like becoming a workaholic and suffering burnout. He won't call you to a frenetic pace that leads to failure. He comforts His sheep with the guidance of His rod and staff. He doesn't drive the flock hard with a cracking whip.

Do you recognize differences in the tone and the intention of each set of voices? We learn to distinguish between the voices in our heads the same way we discern the voices of people we know. Different people sound different. If the voices in our inner thoughts truly come from different sources, they also will differ from one another.

You will learn to recognize God's voice, just as surely as a sheep knows the shepherd. Jesus said, "His sheep follow him because they know his voice" (John 10:4) and "My sheep listen to my voice; I know them, and they follow me" (John 10:27). If sheep can do it, we can too.

Listening

All I have written so far has prepared us for and led to this moment. Now we are ready to start listening for guidance from God.

Carve out some time in your schedule to pause long enough to intentionally listen for direction. God will not usually flag you down in the middle of your hectic day to slow your pace enough for Him to give you input. It helps if you take a moment, preferably in the morning, to get your marching orders for the day.

First, get quiet. God won't talk over us. He's polite. God will strengthen us and allow us to hear Him during times of quietness and rest:

> In repentance and rest is your salvation, in quietness and trust is your strength, but you would have none of it. You said, "No, we will flee on horses." Therefore you will flee!
>
> ISAIAH 30:15-16

We need a time each day when we aren't galloping around all over the place—a time of quiet listening for God to pour refreshing strength and direction into our lives. Intentionally open your heart to guidance, saying, "Lord, You who created all the earth, God of Israel who revealed Yourself to Your people in the Bible, I'm listening to *You* for direction and instruction. Now I'm going to be quiet. Please reveal Yourself and speak to me . . ."

Remember what we learned in the first chapters of this book and the examples of those who walked with God in the Bible? To receive guidance from God will take longer than a standard fifteen-minute quiet time. We will need to invest thirty minutes to an hour or more some days in order to reliably hear guidance from God. The goal for extraordinary hearing is to live your life in a continual guidance loop:

> Pray for marching orders. Hear them. Do them.
> Then pray for more marching orders.

1. Invest at least thirty minutes a day, and often an hour, in concentrated prayer for the people you influence.
2. Pray with a pen and paper nearby and write down the ideas that come to you as you pray for others. This may be God downloading instructions.
3. When you find yourself constantly distracted, pray about the distractions.

4. Ask God for marching orders for the day, write them down, and do them.
5. When you run out of marching orders during the day, pause midday for more marching orders.

Throughout your day, remember to inquire of the Lord about key actions you take. Think back on the first chapters of this book and how important it was for David and other great servants of God to inquire of the Lord. Inquire, for example, before you hit Send on key emails. Jesus can save your soul, but He can also save your job! Don't post something on social media to your hundreds of followers without first inquiring of the Lord.

Our minds are deeply involved in extraordinary hearing. After all, God is speaking thoughts into our *minds*. We need to learn to cooperate with Him in the process.

As I listen, I sometimes sense the Holy Spirit pushing a thought into my mind. As the Holy Spirit impresses His guidance on me, occasionally I need to wait for my mind to form words around the ideas God is giving me. As I learn to more accurately formulate those words, consistent with the idea the Spirit is giving me, I come to "hear" more accurately the "voice" of the Lord.

One key is to learn to have less interference from my own creativity and impulses and leave room for God Himself to dominate my mind. Instead of snatching the steering wheel of my mind away from Him and driving it where I wish He would go, I must learn to stay in tune with the Spirit's leading.

Thinking in God's Presence

Many moments of extraordinary hearing in my life come as I intercede for those I influence. Often during my times of prayer, when I begin interceding for some person or project, I find myself zoning out and thinking about the problems I face related to that person or project. I reflect on challenges and ruminate on potential solutions instead of doing anything that resembles prayer. I may sit there, cogitating, as my hour-long allotted time with the Lord slips by, and then I just keep on thinking as a constellation of ideas starts to form.

In those times of reflection, I fall under the influence of the Holy Spirit's guidance as I grapple with my problems. I call this "thinking in God's presence." With experience, I've learned to differentiate between being distracted and getting an idea from the Lord.

Distractions lead to discouragement and a sense of feeling overwhelmed by details. Ideas from God brighten up my mind with hope and an eagerness to try them out. They provoke the reaction, "Wow, that could change everything!"

I believe Paul was talking about this when he said, "We have the mind of Christ." Having the mind of Christ opens the door for us to comprehend mysteries and instructions that only God can reveal to us. Paul wrote:

> The Spirit searches all things, even the deep things of God. For who knows a person's thoughts except their own spirit within them? In the same way no one knows the thoughts of God except the Spirit of God. What we have received is not the spirit of the world, but the Spirit who is from God, so that we may understand what God has freely given us. This is what we speak, not in words taught us by human wisdom but in words taught by the Spirit, explaining spiritual realities with Spirit-taught words. . . . The person with the Spirit makes judgments about all things, but such

> a person is not subject to merely human judgments, for, "Who has known the mind of the Lord so as to instruct him?" But we have the mind of Christ.
>
> 1 CORINTHIANS 2:10-13, 15-16

I remember a time many years ago when a well-meaning friend fervently prayed for Rebecca and me while repeating over and over, "Lord, please crucify their intellects." As they calmly said "Amen," I desperately wanted to pray a rebuttal.

I don't know why some people think that our minds aren't part of extraordinary hearing and the Christian walk, but I disagree. Paul teaches that the Spirit instructs our *minds* to understand what is happening in the *mind* of God. As the Spirit works in us, He gives us "the *mind* of Christ." If we indeed have the mind of Christ, then we can, as God's Spirit guides us, think of amazing solutions to problems and create incredible new sermons or elegant new organizational structures—all inspired by the mind of Christ.

We need new ideas to make our way through the problems that arise as we serve God. Where do those ideas come from? They can come from God working in our minds. Maybe we cannot overcome the challenge at hand by a simple message from God in a few sentences. Sometimes it requires the development of an entire business model or the unraveling of a budgetary issue.

When faced with a true ministry conundrum, I often take time to think and pray about it. As I pray, I might enter a deep state of reflection. Big ideas often begin to form. Solutions to problems start to evolve in my mind. In this kind of hearing from God, I sometimes get not only words but entire systematic concepts. Whole plans and means of overcoming challenges begin to appear in my mind. Entire outlines of sermons crystalize.

One morning at four o'clock, I woke up unexpectedly with an entire spreadsheet and accompanying bar chart vivid in my mind. I popped out of bed and meticulously typed it all into the computer—one of several divinely assisted spreadsheets I have received during my leadership career. I may not have really received a direct "word of the Lord." It may be more like receiving a download of ideas from God. And leadership depends on great ideas. Who can come up with more powerful ideas than the Creator of the universe?

I don't, however, rush out and proclaim my ideas as irrefutable prophecies. I introduce them cautiously and watch as the body of Christ develops the ideas even further by adding other good thoughts to the mix. It's not that *I* have the mind of Christ individually. Paul says "*we* have the mind of Christ."

The difference between thinking in your own flesh and thinking in the mind of Christ is largely a matter of preparation and intention. It also matters who gets the glory for the ideas. Part of extraordinary hearing therefore includes learning to think in the presence of God.

Discerning and Corroborating

Once you have received what you perceive as a message or idea from God, you need to correctly discern its source. Test the idea to make sure it's completely biblical. Does Scripture resonate with this idea or contradict it? We need to spend time soaking the idea in Scripture to verify its source.

Many have recreated God in their own image and heard from Him only the things that their itching ears longed to hear. Many have proclaimed the prophetic words "peace,

peace" when God proclaimed destruction. We find it easy to have such a great desire for comfort that our minds interfere with the message God wants to speak. We can do that as easily as interrupting someone in conversation. Instead of listening, we find ourselves effortlessly thinking, *In my opinion, what **should** God say right now?*

How can we tell for sure we aren't just making stuff up? Or worse, how can we tell we aren't listening to demonic interruptions or interference? Moses helps us answer that question:

> But you may wonder, "How will we know whether or not a prophecy is from the LORD?" If the prophet speaks in the LORD's name but his prediction does not happen or come true, you will know that the LORD did not give that message. That prophet has spoken without my authority and need not be feared.
>
> DEUTERONOMY 18:21-22, NLT

Early in your attempts to hear from the Lord, test what you believe you are hearing to see if it results in spiritual fruit. If God is really leading, then taking action on that leading will result in eternal impact, not in confusion.

Don't just keep insisting on a specific path; truly be objective and evaluate whether the leading you received *works*. Otherwise, you run the risk of being like the prophets Jeremiah described: "I did not send these prophets, yet they have run with their message; I did not speak to them, yet they have prophesied" (Jeremiah 23:21). The key to discerning the truth of the message is the spiritual benefit that flows out of it. As Jeremiah said,

> "Indeed, I am against those who prophesy false dreams," declares the LORD. "They tell them and lead my people astray with their reckless lies, yet I did not send or appoint them. They do not benefit these people in the least," declares the LORD.
>
> JEREMIAH 23:32

Extraordinary hearing absolutely does not mean depending on your imagination! Ezekiel said, "Thus says the Lord GOD, Woe to the foolish prophets who follow their own spirit, and have seen nothing!" (Ezekiel 13:3, ESV). Ask yourself, "What is the ultimate impact of what I am saying? Does it cause sinners to repent? Does it encourage God's people to continue to serve Him?" If not, beware, because Ezekiel said, "You have discouraged the righteous with your lies, but I didn't want them to be sad. And you have encouraged the wicked by promising them life, even though they continue in their sins" (Ezekiel 13:22, NLT).

Any words you receive from God should lead people closer to Him and to His Word.

It helps if others corroborate the message you believe you have received from God. You probably won't be the only person in your group who is sensitive to the Spirit. Like the church at Antioch, it's better if more than one seasoned follower of Christ comes to the same conclusion about the leading of the Holy Spirit. That heightens the level of confidence we have that the Spirit is speaking to the body of Christ, just as He did in the book of Acts.

Once you have a firm sense that you have correctly discerned what God has communicated to you, then take action consistent with that leading and see what happens. If no spiritual fruit results, you may assume you made a mistake. Along the way, don't assume too much. Admit when you're wrong. Allow for the input of God's leading from others. Learn from your mistakes until you get it right.

Once you have some ministry success based on the guidance of the Holy Spirit, remember that experience. What did that voice sound like in your mind? Learn the voice of the Shepherd. With experience, you can learn to more consistently receive guidance from God.

I've heard people talk about knowing they are in God's will when they have "a sense of peace." They tend to base a lot of their decisions on whether they feel this "peace," but I doubt such a method reliably indicates being in the will of God. The Babylonian king Nebuchadnezzar had loads of peace just before God made him eat grass for seven years (Daniel 4:28-33). Looking for "peace" might also lead you to become unnecessarily risk averse.

I remember one year obeying what I perceived as God's instructions as we tried to purchase land and construct a building. I started the process of doing the due diligence to put the land under contract. Then, before I could sign the contract, I had the opportunity to have the walls of the building framed off-site *for free* by high school volunteers at the International Conference on Missions. I felt certain we could purchase the property before the convention, so I told them to go ahead and build the walls.

I was absolutely wrong about the timing. I'll never forget standing there, surveying the labor at the convention, while hundreds of teenagers thunderously hammered together all the walls for our first building. My eyes scanned all that lumber and all those hardworking kids. All I could think was, *I sure wish I had finished buying that land.* Delays had put me in the unenviable position of having walls but no land to put them on. Staring out at all those walls, I felt grateful, but I did not experience peace.

It all worked out in the end. But if I had insisted on taking only those actions that gave me peace, I would have done none of that!

As I write, I'm sitting in that building on that land. I now have the peace that passes understanding. But as I followed God's leading for my life, I was a long way from having peace about it.

Action often entails risk. Looking back over the years of my life, I see that if I had insisted on feeling peace whenever I had discerned God's leading, I never would have taken many good, God-inspired risks.

Having peace from God is nice when you can get it, but that shouldn't mean that anything that makes you nervous disqualifies such direction as God's leading for you. More often than not, God's plan will scare the fool out of you.

Watch for multiple corroborations of the message. Take action and stay alert for opportunities consistent with what you perceive as God's message. Listen regularly for further refinement of the message. When it "works," remember to learn what that directive "voice" felt like in your mind. Pray in ways consistent with achieving the direction of the message. Learn by observing which prayers God answers and which prayers He doesn't. Adjust your understanding based on what God will truly do in answer to your prayers. Distinguish between your mind's voice, Satan's voice, and God's voice. This all takes experience.

What Is Too Hard for God?

Let's go back and finish the story of My Father's World, the business-turned-mission owned by my friends David and Marie. Remember how God doubled their spiritual impact by spreading their work around the world, all the while allowing their customer base to erode in 2018 and 2019?

That's not where God ended the story.

When March 2020 rolled around, the COVID-19 pandemic slammed into the whole world. The entire United States of America suddenly found itself sheltering in place. School got forced back into the home for a time.

All at once, a huge resurgence of interest in homeschool curricula spread instantaneously around the nation. The number of leads on new customers exploded by orders of magnitude. In 2020, My Father's World dramatically increased its customer base, just as the group had prayed—doubling many metrics in that single year. It looked impossible, but with God, all things are possible. God can see pandemics coming!

When we start listening to God and praying the kinds of prayers that He promises to answer with unlimited power, all things under His guidance truly are possible.

If God can work through a pandemic to answer our prayers, then what is too hard for God to do? Nothing is too hard for Him!

And remember that the whole idea of "doubling" started with Marie Hazell quietly cultivating her heart with spiritual habits. She invested daily time getting quiet and listening for God's direction for her. She heard the word "double" from God. The staff of My Father's World collaborated to create that strategic prayer request list. David Hazell provided the leadership of assimilating and integrating the list. The whole staff gathered to lift up persistent, unified group prayer. And God heard their prayers and decided to cover Himself in glory.

It takes work! We must build the habits that open the door for God to speak into our lives. We must cultivate the skill of extraordinary hearing. But in the final analysis, *you* can do this.

Why not start today?

Discussion Questions

1. How do *you* experience voices speaking in your mind?
2. Have you ever concluded that a thought in your mind was put there by a demon? How could you tell?
3. Have you ever heard a thought in your mind that seemed to be spoken by God? How could you tell?
4. How do you test and evaluate your thoughts?
5. What experience do you have of receiving dreams or visual pictures from God?
6. What experience do you have "thinking in the presence of God"?
7. How do you inquire of the Lord in your life? About what kinds of decisions?

EPILOGUE

GLORY

Those who are victorious will sit with me on my throne.

REVELATION 3:21, NLT

THERE ONCE WAS a man who ran a vineyard in Napa Valley. At the crack of dawn, he rushed into town to buy some groceries and pick up a group of day laborers to work the harvest. The workday got off to a great start as beautiful, ripe mounds of grape clusters began to pile up, filling huge, white tubs strategically placed all around the vineyard. Everything seemed to be coming together.

At 9 a.m., he raced back into town to buy something at the hardware store, only to find people standing around with nothing to do: unemployed, purposeless men and women just loitering around. Forcefully interrupting their day, he hired them on the spot and sped them along to work in his vineyard.

A few hours later, around lunchtime, some equipment broke, and he had to rush back into town to pick up a replacement part. There again, he saw more idle workers, just hanging around; he hired them too. And then once more, a few hours later at three o'clock, the same thing happened.

As the time to knock off work for the day approached, he had to scramble back into town on yet another errand, where once more he stumbled across still another group of people lounging around, completely idle. Stunned, he sputtered, "Why are you standing around here wasting the whole day, doing absolutely nothing?" (Matthew 20:6, GPT).

"Nobody's hired us," they answered. And they, too, got vacuumed up into the service of the vineyard.

Jesus paints Himself in this self-portrait as a man with an unquenchable passion for grapes who simply can't stand to see anyone not reaping fruit. He passes from task to task with great intentionality, flabbergasted every time He stumbles across someone not already totally focused on producing grapes. He sweeps through the marketplace, practically abducting everyone who hasn't managed to find a purpose in life.

Has His passion for producing eternal fruit captured you? When you prepare your heart to properly hear from Jesus, He won't leave you without a purpose. Like the man from the vineyard, He will sweep into your life without fail and put you to work with the goal of helping you fulfill your created purpose.

My fellow workers, the sun is setting on our day in the vineyard—the end approaches. Get ready!

Train to Reign

Extraordinary hearing matters *forever*.

The Bible insists that one day we will reign in heaven with Christ. What if this life is just work experience bearing fruit that qualifies us for reigning with Jesus? Maybe we're just building our résumés!

I had always assumed that heaven would be great because it's a magical place where God finally obligates people to behave themselves. And it is true that we won't have the cravings of our fallen physical bodies anymore. But wouldn't it be much more typical of God's nature not to *force* us to behave well but to train and shape us to become great at what we need to be in heaven?

Heaven will be heaven because God will place the greatest servant leaders in all of history in charge of meeting each and every need. He will place in positions of responsibility the greatest multicultural, humble, skilled leaders of all time—each one under the uncontested power and direction of the resurrected Jesus. *That's* heaven!

The purpose of this life, and the reason it's important for us to learn to walk with God and hear Him speak, is that He can make us into what we need to be so that heaven will be what heaven needs to be. There's more at stake here than we realize!

No shortcuts exist to honing the soul of a great servant leader. God forges in us the character needed to reign with Christ, by helping us patiently endure all the painful chapters of this life. We ourselves are the treasure that God is sculpting for Himself to enjoy eternally in heaven.

Whenever we hear guidance from the Spirit and obey, you and I are preparing to reign with Christ. Life is short, but we *can* seek eternity while we are here. Wise people will invest these fleeting moments to become skilled at participating in eternity—while they still can.

Learning extraordinary hearing now prepares us for that brilliant future. To qualify, we must have an ingrained habit of obedience to Jesus. We build that habit here. Heaven will not offer on-the-job training; there's too much at stake by that point.

Experience on earth has eternal worth. If we suffer for a time here, and if that suffering creates a greater capacity to make heaven wonderful, then it's worth it. God doesn't waste our pain. We suffer and genuinely struggle on earth, but maybe that struggle provides the only pathway to get spiritually refined. The math works. Eighty years of toil gains eighty gazillion years of beauty, grace, and wonder—peacefully thriving and reigning with God in His presence.

What about You?

So, what about you? Are you learning to become what heaven needs you to be? Take a hard look at your life's résumé. Do you have any relevant work experience? God is looking to hire you to reign with Christ. That's what Jesus means when he talks about our reward in heaven. He rewards us with a unique future, a significant role in making heaven great. *Now* is the time to get some hands-on experience in the things of heaven.

When you learn to hear guidance from Jesus and obey Him, you will be ready. Don't worry. It doesn't depend on you alone. Jesus is powerful enough to get you ready.

You matter. You matter *forever*. You might refuse to believe that you could be called to reign with Christ. You might feel tempted to say, "No, you are wrong. I'm nothing. I'm not great. I could never be that." But wait a minute! Remember the point of the parable about the grapes: "So the last will be first" (Matthew 20:16).

What if Jesus is looking for people like *you*—and not the people celebrated in this world? It's not far-fetched. What if simple ministries like teaching children in Sunday school build the *exact* skills and character needed to patiently care for people in heaven? I would pick my elementary Sunday school teacher to reign over me rather than a celebrity. She had the patience of Job! At least I would know that snack time and nap time would be glorious.

Yes, you *are* in the running. You are *in* this job interview. So get ready for the Day!

Watch for Jesus' Return

Can you picture that day of His return? You will *see* the resurrected Jesus in all His blinding glory and fall at His feet, overwhelmed by His radiant face. You will *feel* the scars on his nail-pierced hand as He reaches down to comfort you with a gentle, reassuring touch. "Do not be afraid," He will softly say, with tears of emotion pooling in His compassionate eyes. "I am the First and the Last. I am the Living One; I was dead, and now look, I am alive for ever and ever! And I hold the keys of death and Hades" (Revelation 1:17-18).

You will feel the scratch of His beard as He pulls you in close and lovingly smooths away the salty tears running down your cheeks. Then, at just the right moment, He will turn and usher you to your rightful place in the new creation.

"Look, My child! For all this time, I've been preparing this place for you, and you for this place." Then you and the people you love will shine like stars for all eternity. Every day that passes moves you one day further from death—not closer. And you will reign forever and ever in perfect harmony with Christ Himself.

Yes, it's worth it! So listen. Walk with God. Learn to hear His voice and obey.

And get ready for glory!

Discussion Questions

1. What future role in heaven does your current life prepare you to do?

2. How do you think making disciples of all the languages and cultures on earth would prepare people to reign in heaven?

3. How does serving people here prepare you to serve in heaven?

4. Now that you have read this whole book, what has changed in your life along the way as you applied what you read?

5. What has God begun to say to you?

6. What do you sense God teaching you about your purpose?

7. What first steps do you plan to take to fulfill that purpose?

ACKNOWLEDGMENTS

It takes a village to write a book. My name gets published on the front, but a boatload of others contribute.

To my astonishing colleagues in Pioneer Bible Translators scattered over the earth: Thank you for helping me grow spiritually and giving me the community in which to learn the voice of the Shepherd. It is the greatest privilege of my life to wake up every day trying to figure out how to serve you. Leaders should inspire followers, but in my case, it is you who have inspired me. Someday I hope to learn how to lead as well as your sacrificial lifestyles of service to Christ would deserve. Thank you especially to my dozens of teammates who meticulously studied the manuscript, adding copious notes to un-muddle my ideas.

To the whole Yalunka people and my Yalunka brothers and sisters in Christ: May God bless you richly for radically reframing the world for me. You gave me the opportunity to learn to hear from God in a way that I could only encounter living far from home. Thank you for sharing your precious language and culture with me. Thank you for taking care of me and my family while we lived in your neighborhood.

To the board of directors of Pioneer Bible Translators: Thank you for authorizing me to invest time in this writing project.

To my publisher, Tyndale: Thank you so much, Sarah Atkinson

and Christina Garrison, for giving this book a chance. Thank you also, Steve Halliday, for your editorial horsepower and for drawing on the richness of your communication expertise to make this book so much better. At one time, I wondered how Tyndale consistently publishes the work of such good authors. Now I understand that Tyndale makes the authors good. Thank you for investing in high-powered editing to hone my skills. You all are phenomenal!

NOTES

1. *Merriam-Webster*, s.v. "extraordinary" and "hearing," accessed August 30, 2022, https://www.merriam-webster.com/dictionary/extraordinary and https://www.merriam-webster.com/dictionary/hearing.
2. See textual footnote to Isaiah 8:1 in the NIV.
3. My daughter taught me to watch for this theme in the Bible.
4. For more information, check out https://www.perspectives.org/.
5. To find out more about unreached people groups around the world, see https://joshuaproject.net/.
6. William L. Holladay, ed., *A Concise Hebrew and Aramaic Lexicon of the Old Testament* (Grand Rapids, MI: Eerdmans, 1988), 356.
7. 1 Samuel 22:10; 1 Samuel 23:2; 1 Samuel 23:4; 1 Samuel 30:8; 2 Samuel 2:1; 2 Samuel 5:19; 2 Samuel 5:23; 1 Chronicles 14:10; 1 Chronicles 14:14.
8. See Simon Bartz,"Full Bible Translation Tops 700 Languages for First Time," Bible Society, updated October 4, 2021, https://www.biblesociety.org.uk/latest/news/full-bible-translation-tops-700-languages-for-first-time/.
9. Holladay, *Concise Hebrew and Aramaic Lexicon*, 254.
10. Charles Duhigg, *The Power of Habit: Why We Do What We Do in Life and Business* (New York: Random House, 2012), 17–18.
11. John C. Maxwell, *The 15 Invaluable Laws of Growth* (New York: Center Street, 2014), xiv.
12. The mission of Faith Comes By Hearing is to provide the Word of God in audio and video format to people groups around the world. Find out more at https://www.faithcomesbyhearing.com/.
13. To learn more about disciple-making movements, read Doug Lucas, *More Disciples: A Guide to Becoming and Multiplying Followers of Jesus* (Monument, CO: WIGTake Resources, 2019).
14. The Hebrew word translated "holy" means "to be set apart" (Abridged

Brown-Driver-Briggs Hebrew-English lexicon of the Old Testament). The Greek means the same: "things set apart for God's purpose" (Analytical Lexicon of the Greek New Testament).

15. "Gunman Opens Fire on Las Vegas Concert Crowd, Wounding Hundreds and Killing 58," History.com, updated September 28, 2021, https://www.history.com/this-day-in-history/2017-las-vegas-shooting. See also Jennifer Medina, "A New Report on the Las Vegas Gunman Was Released. Here Are Some Takeaways," *The New York Times*, January 19, 2018, https://www.nytimes.com/2018/01/19/us/las-vegas-attack-shooting-paddock.html.
16. "US Religious Landscape Survey: Religious Beliefs and Practices," Pew Research Center, June 1, 2008, https://www.pewresearch.org/religion/2008/06/01/u-s-religious-landscape-survey-religious-beliefs-and-practices/.
17. The Bible also mentions dedicating a home in Deuteronomy 20:5.
18. To see what sign language Scripture looks like, visit https://deaf.bible/.
19. See https://deaf.pioneerbible.org/. See also David L. Thomas, "Bible Translators Add 400 Sign Languages to To-Do List," *Christianity Today*, January 3, 2022, https://www.christianitytoday.com/news/2022/january/deaf-bible-translation-400-2033-illuminations-pioneer.html.
20. Find out more about this ministry at https://www.deafmissions.com/.
21. Discover more about this collaborative effort at https://illuminations.bible/.
22. Author of *The One Thing You Need to Know: . . . About Great Managing, Great Leading, and Sustained Individual Success* (London: Simon and Schuster, 2005).
23. See their website at https://www.mfwbooks.com.
24. Check out the Bible reading plan of Journey: Life Transforming Conversations with God at https://www.journeyeveryday.com/.
25. An audacious prayer would ask for doubling every five years, a 14 percent annual growth rate. Usually, praying for a 7 to 10 percent increase per year is a healthy target long-term.
26. "When Americans Say They Believe in God, What Do They Mean?" Pew Research Center, Religion and Public Life, April 25, 2018, https://www.pewresearch.org/religion/2018/04/25/when-americans-say-they-believe-in-god-what-do-they-mean/.
27. Russell T. Hurlburt, Christopher L. Heavey, and Jason M. Kelsey, "Toward a Phenomenology of Inner Speaking," *Consciousness and Cognition* 22, no. 4, (2013): 1477–94, http://dx.doi.org/10.1016/j.concog.2013.10.003.

ABOUT THE AUTHOR

GREG PRUETT has served as president of Pioneer Bible Translators, based in Dallas, Texas, since January 2007. Before that, Greg, along with his wife, Rebecca, and their three children, lived in West Africa for more than twelve years, where they completed a translation of the entire Bible into the Yalunka language and shared Christ's love with people who traditionally follow the Quran. During regular visits to West Africa, Greg and Rebecca continue to work with the Yalunka church to learn together to multiply disciples and plant churches in every village and among the surrounding unreached people groups. Greg has a degree in civil engineering from Texas A&M and both a master's degree and a PhD from Fuller Theological Seminary.